TOURISM, BIODIVERSITY AND SUSTAINABLE DEVELOPMENT

TOURISM, BIODIVERSITY AND SUSTAINABLE DEVELOPMENT

(In 6 Volumes)

Assessing Tourism: Impacts in Asia and Pacific

(Volume 3)

Editor

Prof. O.P. KANDARI
ASHISH CHANDRA

ISHA BOOKS
DELHI—110 033

Tourism, Biodiversity and Sustainable Development
(Tourism/Culture)

Rs. 5000 (Set in 6 Vols.)
Rs. 850 (Each Volume)

ISBN: 81-8205-033-2 (Set)
ISBN: 81-8205-036-7 (Vol. 3)

Published in 2004 in India by
Isha Books, D-43, Prithviraj Road
Adarsh Nagar, Delhi-110 033

Lasertypesetting by: Varsha Graphics, Delhi
Printed at: Chawla Offset Press, Delhi

Contents

Preface

Tourism is now one of the fastest growing sectors of the economies of many countries as it assumes a dominant role in the service sector. It is astonishing to note that in a short span of fifty years, tourism has fast grown up as a pursuit of profound human interest, developing itself as the world's most important industry in terms of export earnings. World recognizes tourism as an industry for generating immense business opportunities, a creator of wealth, income multiplier, a catalyst for employment and preserver of culture and environment. In this ever-changing dynamic world, tourism has shown a remarkable and sustained growth both as an activity as well as an industry in almost all the geographical areas of the world.

It is well known that as a contributor to the global economy, tourism has no equal. The figures denoting the fast growth of tourism sector quoted in the report of World Tourism and Travel Council (WTTC) are worth mentioning. Tourism employs 10.6% of the global workforce and contributes 10.2% to world's GDP. It generates tax revenue of $ 655 billion and is the largest industry with $3.4 trillion gross output. It is interesting to note that all studies connected with tourism and aviation suggest that the focus of travel and tourism is gradually but deliberately shifting from Europe and North America to East/South Asia and the Pacific. The WTCC Tourism Satellite Account 2001 confirms this phenomenon and has projected data of far reaching implications for Indian tourism in the coming decade.

The rapid growth of tourism in Asia and the Pacific has raised a number of interrelated issues that challenge the effectiveness and efficiency of government. In this region, tourism is generally considered to be an economic activity, but sustainable tourism development involves almost all aspects of life. Therefore, the tourism industry must be viewed as an integrated whole with an impact on the economy, society, culture and the physical environment. Government policy makers and all stakeholders in the tourism sector must work together to meet present needs without compromising the ability of future generations to meet their own needs.

This book attempts assess the current trends of tourism development in the Asia Pacific region. The chapters in this book explains the task of achieving tourism growth in harmony with sustainability considerations and in particular spatial and cultural contexts of Asia and Pacific.

Editor

1

Sustainable Tourism in Asia and Pacific

Since the United Nations Conference on Environment and Development held at Rio de Janeiro in 1992, a set of principles, goals and activities leading to sustainable development was endorsed by signatory nations. The role of governments in implementing Agenda 21: Programme of Action for Sustainable Development emphasized that sustainability involved policy and planning, integrated decision-making and community participation. Agenda 21 also gave impetus to greater efforts aimed at spelling out the importance of sustainable development in the tourism sector. In the Asian and Pacific region, member countries and areas of Economic and Social Commission for Asia and Pacific (ESCAP) have been addressing various issues related to sustainable tourism development since the mid-1990s. At a number of ESCAP meetings, particularly since the Intergovernmental Meeting on Tourism Development held in 1996, decisions and recommendations related to tourism's contribution to development focused on the need for a comprehensive framework for action at national and regional levels.

At its fifty-third session in 1997, the Commission suggested that a plan of action should provide the framework for effective cooperation and promotion of tourism by member countries and areas. More specifically, the plan of action should focus on strengthening national capabilities and promoting regional cooperation in sustainable tourism development. The Commission, at its fifty-fifth session in April 1999, adopted the Plan of Action for Sustainable Tourism Development in the Asian and Pacific Region (PASTA). PASTA aims to ensure long-term prosperity in Asia and the Pacific by increasing the contribution of tourism through responsible action by governments and stakeholders at the national level, with supporting action at the regional level in order to bring benefits to wide segments of society. The intention is to implement PASTA within a five-year timeframe from 1999 to 2005. Following its adoption, the World Tourism Organization (WTO) and several other international organizations involved in tourism have expressed their willingness to cooperate in the implementation of PASTA.

Since 1999, ESCAP-member countries and areas have been taking action at the national level to implement PASTA. Various international and regional organizations have been providing support through actions at the regional level. There are six main theme areas identified in PASTA for action by governments and other stakeholders in the tourism sector.

Plan of Action for Sustainable Tourism

The objective of PASTA is to increase the contribution of tourism to national social and economic development in ways that sustain people's prosperity in the short and long term. Tourism is generally considered to be an economic activity, but PASTA asserts that sustainable tourism development involves almost all aspects of life. Therefore, the tourism industry must be viewed as an integrated whole with an impact on the economy, society, culture and the physical environment. Government policy makers and all stakeholders in the tourism sector must work together to meet present needs without compromising the ability of future generations to meet their own needs.

The rapid growth of tourism in Asia and the Pacific has raised a number of interrelated issues that challenge the effectiveness and efficiency of government, and these are covered as the parameters for PASTA.

The first issue involves tourism policy-making in both its substantive and procedural aspects. A country's tourism policy should provide the most explicit statement of the government's approach to sustainable tourism development and the roles that all stakeholders in the tourism sector are expected to take. In order for policy-making to be effective, government policy-makers and stakeholders need reliable information and timely data of good quality to enable better understanding of tourism's complex and long-term interactions with the rest of the economy. The effectiveness of tourism policy-making will clearly be influenced by the availability of resources.

The second issue relates to planning in terms of its policy and operational elements as part of a process for deciding objectives, priorities and means for achieving objectives. Sustainable tourism development can be achieved in a comprehensive way through the use of a tourism master plan as well as integrated tourism planning. In addition, planning based on reliable and timely information can highlight the links between national economic development and the tourism sector.

The third issue concerns management for sustainable tourism development, which involves leading, coordinating and controlling actions to mobilize resources in order to formulate and implement tourism policies and plans. This also involves administrative issues about the structure, functions and responsibilities of the national tourism organization. At a more general level, management issues involve working arrangements between the government and other tourism stakeholders, coherent intersectoral coordination, promotion of broader participation and arrangements to facilitate spreading the benefits of tourism more widely.

The fourth issue focuses on participation of the private sector as a major stakeholder providing tourism services. This involves questions about how to attract greater private sector participation that is appropriate for sustainable tourism development as well as how to encourage public and private sector partnerships. Government policies and plans would need to focus on creation of a conducive business environment, formulation of an adequate legislative framework and strengthened governmental capacities to work with the private sector to make sustainable tourism development the top priority.

PASTA contains proposals for action at the national level along with supporting actions at the regional level with the aim of strengthening national capabilities and promoting regional cooperation in sustainable tourism development. This provides the framework for ESCAP-member countries and areas to review progress and identify obstacles. The six theme areas also serve as the framework for reviewing the support programmes and projects undertaken by international and regional organizations, including ESCAP.

1. Human resources development in the tourism sector

As a result of growth in the tourism industry and its priority for economic development in a number of countries and areas, developing the required human resources who will provide tourism services has become vital for sustainability. Many countries and areas in Asia and the Pacific lack strategies and policies designed to develop human resources for the tourism sector. Some specific concerns include:

(a) the quantity and quality of human resources for a sector that is labour intensive and requires a high standard of specialized skills in cross-cultural working environments;

(b) the shortage of tourism training infrastructure and qualified trainers in many countries; and

(c) the lack of national legislation or guidelines to improve working conditions and career opportunities in the tourism sector.

In this context, the following actions are proposed:

(a) Actions at the national level

(i) Governments should assess present and future training requirements for human resources development.

(ii) Governments should consider formulating national strategies for tourism training and human resources development.

(iii) Each country should establish a national tourism training committee consisting of representatives from the government, training institutes and the tourism industry.

(iv) Each country should consider active participation in the Network of Asia-Pacific Education and Training Institutes in Tourism (APETIT).

(v) Each country should consider setting up a national network of tourism education and training institutes to further strengthen cooperation.

(b) Supporting actions at the regional level

(i) ESCAP, WTO and other international and regional organizations involved in tourism should extend their full support to ensure effective operation of APETIT with a view to promoting human resources development in many countries.

2. *Economic impact of tourism*

While there is a general awareness of the economic benefits of tourism, its net contribution to the economy is often not known, making it difficult to make effective policies. Systematic research to understand the economic impact of tourism is needed to:

(a) make integrated planning easier,

(b) strengthen links between national economic development policy-making and sustainable tourism development and

(c) better understand how to maximize the economic benefits from tourism. Countries could also learn from studying each other's experiences with enhancing the economic benefits of tourism.

Proposed actions that could be taken are:

(a) Actions at the national level

(i) Countries that have already made studies of the economic impact of tourism should continuously update their data and research, and use these findings to establish an appropriate role for tourism in the national economy.

(ii) Countries which have not yet studied the economic impact of tourism should undertake such research/ studies to be able to establish appropriate policies for tourism development.

(b) Supporting actions at the regional level

(i) Seminars and workshops should be organized to strengthen country capabilities to use different methodologies for determining economic impact, including the WTO's global methodology, tourism satellite account; and WTO could provide its expertise in support of country and regional studies.

(ii) ESCAP, which prepared Guidelines on Input-Output Analysis of Tourism, could assist countries in measuring the economic impact of tourism using the input-output technique, through advisory services or organization of national workshops.

3. *Environmental management of tourism*

The complex relationship between development and its impact on the environment creates problems for the effective environmental management of tourism development. Effective planning and coordination, as well as efficient enforcement of legislation can help address the problems.

Efforts at environmental management should include coordinating strategies at all levels and among many sectors; making appropriate use of resources; and creating greater awareness of environmental consequences. Problems with legislation relate to enforcement of laws, the need for human resources to monitor and enforce and the need for stakeholders to understand the long-term benefits for sustainability if they comply with environmental laws and policies. Sustainability also involves balancing tourism development with preserving the environment, the cultural heritage and indigenous cultures of local communities.

In this context, the following actions could be taken:

(a) Actions at the national level

(i) Governments should give more attention to planning, coordination and monitoring of tourism development and environmental management.

(ii) Local communities should have greater involvement in environmental management and sustainable tourism development.

(iii) Governments should create awareness through the mass media, among the general public and international tourists about protecting and preserving the environment in order to sustain tourism.

(iv) Countries should pay particular attention to development and promotion of ecotourism.

(b) Supporting actions at the regional level

(i) Seminars and workshops should be organized in order to facilitate sharing of experiences and information for developing ecotourism.

(ii) Technical cooperation among countries should be promoted through exchange visits of experts on technical aspects of environmental management of sustainable tourism development.

4. *Infrastructure development and investment for the tourism sector*

The relationship between infrastructure development and sustainable tourism development becomes clear once policy-makers and planners see that inadequate infrastructure is one of the most serious constraints to future prospects for tourism development. Integrated planning and the use of master plans can help overcome many constraints. In addition, the government should create an environment conducive to private sector investment, which may also include investment incentives. Infrastructure requirements for the tourism sector should be properly integrated with the full range of a country's infrastructure development and investment requirements.

To this end, the following actions are proposed:

(a) Actions at the national level

(i) Governments should indicate clear commitments about private sector involvement in tourism infrastructure development, and this should form part of integrated plans or a master plan.

(ii) In order to attract private sector participation, governments should address such issues as creating a conducive business environment, liberalizing rules and regulations, providing investment incentives, developing an adequate legislative framework and strengthening governmental capacity to negotiate.

(iii) National workshops should be organized to build capabilities among government officials in negotiating techniques and in promoting partnership between the public and private sector in order to develop tourism and related infrastructure.

(b) Supporting actions at the regional level

(i) World Bank, Asian Development Bank and other development financing institutions should extend full assistance to tourism infrastructure development.

(ii) Seminars and workshops should be organized on tourism infrastructure development and investment involving policy-makers, investors, national tourism organizations and other government agencies in order to share experiences among countries at different stages of tourism development.

(iii) Training workshops should be organized to build capabilities among government officials in negotiating technique and to promote relationships between the public and private sector for tourism and related infrastructure development.

5. *Facilitation of travel*

A wide range of travel facilitation problems can impede sustainable tourism development. These problems can include, among others:

(a) lack of accessibility;

(b) inefficient policies and procedures for visas, customs and currency;

(c) possible threats to the health and safety of tourists;

(d) lack of information services for tourists;

(e) negative image if there is overpricing; and

(f) the complex nature of border formalities and customs regulations.

Governments have a direct role in making policies, rules and regulations and providing related infrastructure.

In this context, the following actions could be taken:

(a) Actions at the national level

(i) Each country should set up an interministerial committee/council, including representatives from the tourism industry, to promote coordinated development of tourism and facilitation of travel.

(ii) Each country should consider setting up a consultative council comprised of the tourism and aviation industries to consider accessibility issues by sharing views and harmonizing divergent interests.

(iii) Countries should conduct training programmes for immigration and customs officials to make needed changes and take required actions in order to improve efficiency and courtesy.

(iv) Countries should develop national policies on tourists' health and safety and provide tourists with appropriate information upon arrival.

(b) Supporting actions at the regional level

(i) Regional seminars should be organized to share experiences and learn from the best practices within and outside the region.

(ii) ESCAP should undertake land transport corridor studies along major routes to identify barriers to tourist travel and suggest remedial measures.

(iii) WTO and other concerned international and regional organizations should provide information and training on safety, security and health standards for tourists and encourage countries to share experiences in developing a multilateral agreement on safety and security standards.

6. Regional and subregional cooperation in tourism development

Countries and areas in the Asian and Pacific region and different subregions may have limited accessibility, lack resources and/or capabilities or have inadequate arrangement for expanding tourism. Regional and subregional cooperation could help to more effectively address many problems if countries and areas shared information, facilities, experiences and expertise. Such cooperation would promote sustainable tourism development by conserving scarce resources, increasing cultural and economic understanding, increase the frequency of international contacts and exchanges and reduce unnecessary competition. A number of existing regional and subregional arrangements could provide the basis for initiating cooperation to promote sustainable tourism, namely:

Association of South East Asian Nations (ASEAN), the South Asian Association for Regional Cooperation (SAARC), Asia-Pacific Economic Cooperation (APEC), Indian Ocean, the Greater Mekong subregion, Bangladesh-India-Myanmar-Sri Lanka-Thailand Economic Cooperation (BIMST-EC), Tumen River area, the Pacific islands, and among countries along the Silk Road and the Asian Highway.

The following actions could be taken:

(a) Actions at the national level

(i) Governments should actively participate in the existing cooperative groupings with a view to contribute to regional and subregional tourism development and to benefit from sharing and collaboration.

(ii) Governments should take initiatives to strengthen bilateral/ multilateral cooperative arrangements for sustainable tourism development and promotion.

(b) Supporting actions at the regional level

(i) ESCAP, WTO and other international and regional organizations should make concerted efforts in areas of their special competence to promote regional and subregional cooperation, as well as to strengthen national capabilities in sustainable tourism development.

(ii) Some mechanisms that could be considered by these agencies in promoting regional and subregional cooperation may include organization of regional and subregional meetings and seminars and conducting studies.

Modalities for implementation

One or more modalities may facilitate successful implementation of the various actions listed above. Effective implementation of PASTA would require a fundamental review of policy-making, planning, managing and defining private sector participation for the purpose of sustainable tourism development. Governments and regional organizations are encouraged to be innovative in preparing approaches that make use of national and regional resources.

Governments would generally be responsible for action at the country level, while action at the regional level has been designed to support and facilitate. Supporting action at the regional level could include technical assistance; regional research and development, including comparative studies; opportunities to exchange experiences and know-how; and cooperation and facilitation of sustainable tourism development activities that are expected to have an impact transcending nation borders.

A number of modalities are presented in order to see that the consequences of actions could be far-reaching in the socio-economic and environmental terms that define sustainable tourism development. The following modalities could enable implementation of proposed actions at the national level:

(a) *National policy coordination committee for sustainable tourism development*: Collaboration is needed at the highest national level where policy is developed, formulated and coordinated. The main roles of the committee would be to (i) provide a framework for integrated tourism planning or master plans, (ii) harmonize strategies and (iii) propose consolidation of resources from various tourism-related ministries and agencies. The purpose of a national policy coordination committee is to attain sustainable tourism objectives in an efficient way.

(b) *Public/private sector consultative committees*: The private sector, including business enterprises and non-governmental organizations (NGOs), are already involved in many areas of sustainable tourism development. Consultative committees are one type of modality enabling the government to maintain constructive dialogues and have multiple sources of information to help in policy-making, planning and management.

(c) *Facilitation committees*: Sustainable tourism development requires harmonious interactions involving parties from both the public and private sectors. They will need to work together, especially when difficult issues are raised, when the needs of various government ministries may differ and when various short-term objectives might create disagreements. Implementation also requires collaboration among various groups and organizations. Facilitation committees are one type of modality for resolving problems and issues at the working level. Such committees can contribute to improved productivity and reduction of costs.

(d) *Interdisciplinary teams*: People from specialized fields with unique experiences are valuable resources and can contribute to sustainable tourism development through the synergies created by their collaboration. Such interdisciplinary teams could be organized for special, time-bound tasks that will contribute to the process of sustainable tourism development.

(e) *Sustainable development zones*: The creation of such zones in different parts of the country provides opportunities to focus efforts and formulate experimental/pilot projects for sustainable tourism development. Development zones allow for innovative approaches and can serve as experiments before full implementation.

(f) *Demonstration projects for sustainable tourism development*: Demonstration projects at the local and community levels can serve to test legal and regulatory reforms, innovations in administration and the dynamics of public participation to make tourism development sustainable. This modality could work for small-scale projects and activities, but they could be adjusted to the national level after their success was demonstrated.

A number of modalities could be used at the regional level to provide support or serve as the catalyst that encourages the process of sustainable tourism development. The following regional modalities have been identified as appropriate for implementation of PASTA:

(a) sharing information, research and data;

(b) making comparative studies in sustainable tourism development;

(c) supporting technical cooperation among developing countries (TCDC); and

(d) encouraging regional and subregional cooperation, especially through existing organizations and forums.

Progress and obstacles in implementing PASTA

The progress and obstacles in selected countries or areas for implementing PASTA at the national level are discussed below.

Armenia

There is strong potential for sustainable tourism development in Armenia, because there are many tourist attractions, including the landscape, cultural and historical heritage, unique architecture and friendly hospitality of Armenian people. The Tourism Development Department of the Ministry of Industry and Trade has identified ecotourism and spa tourism as promising areas for tourism development. Over the past few years, it was reported that tourism has been the fastest growing economic sector, notwithstanding serious constraints caused by political conflict in the region and a recent natural disaster due to an earthquake. Given the geo-political position of Armenia, it is directly affected when neighbouring countries close trade and travel routes. Despite these circumstances, since 1994 international tourism has grown steadily from 13,000 visitors in 1996 to 48,000 visitors in 2000. Plans for 2001 related to national events celebrating 1,700 years of Christianity forecast that the number of tourists would reach 100,000.

Armenia's national actions in the six theme areas of PASTA should be viewed in terms of the growing contribution of tourism to national economic development and the idea that natural and cultural attractions favour large-scale tourism development. The national tourism organization (NTO) has given special attention to human resources development. A training programme focused on the most crucial job specializations in tourism is part of the newly developed five-year master plan "State Programme on Tourism Development in Armenia" (2000-2005). The NTO has recently organized several national tourism training and education activities. Emphasis is also given to participation in international training activities as part of technical assistance programmes. There are plans to establish a tourism school in Armenia with bilateral assistance from the Government of France.

The economic impact of tourism is well recognized as the engine of growth for the Armenian economy. Tourism is the main source of foreign exchange earnings and contributed about US$ 48 million to the economy in 2000. It was estimated that direct and indirect employment in the tourism industry covered about 14,000 jobs in 1998. Standard statistics about hotel occupancy rates, international tourism receipts and regional distribution of tourists throughout the country are readily available. However, a complete and full assessment of the economic impact has been hindered by data limitations and lack of funds to make such evaluations.

In the area of environmental management of tourism, several state bodies are empowered to protect and preserve the natural environment as well as man-made sites and monuments of archeological and historical importance. The NTO collaborates with the Ministry of Ecology and Preservation of Nature and the Directorate of Heritage Preservation, including making draft laws for particular sites and areas, such as national parks. The United Nations Education, Science and Culture Organization (UNESCO) has worked with the government to help preserve and enhance important sites for cultural tourism. Currently, UNESCO has designated the monasteries of Haghpat and Sanahin as world heritage sites. There are plans to add nine other heritage sites. However, almost all archeological and historical sites need substantial repair and maintenance.

Action in Armenia related to infrastructure development and investment for the tourism sector focused on improving the investment climate and accelerating the process of privatization. A new investment law was recently issued to give incentives and privileges to both local and foreign private investors, with special attention to the tourism sector. Between 1997 and 2000, there were 18 tourist investment projects approved, mostly for establishing hotels.

The road network, as well as public and private ground transport, is generally in good condition. The Ministry of Industry and Trade has submitted a concept/ project proposal to the Minister on Regional Governance on the establishment of tourism infrastructure, including tourism routes and various infrastructure projects. Private investment in infrastructure development is encouraged by policies that supply land at nominal prices and provide soft loans.

Facilitation of travel has been encouraged in part by economic reforms and good relations with the countries that are major tourist markets, particularly the United States and countries of Western Europe. The only international airport in Armenia has been remodeled and expanded to receive flights from a number of major cities in Europe, North America, the Commonwealth of Independent States (CIS) and the Middle East. Access by land through the borders with some neighbouring countries can be problematic during periods of political conflict or internal instability. The government has been considering proposals to reduce visa fees, streamline visa procedures, facilitate customs procedures and reduce airline prices.

Armenia has been active in areas of regional and subregional cooperation, especially within the framework of the WTO programme on the Great Silk Road. In 1999, the First Caucasus International Fair was held along with a conference on "Peaceful Caucasus". There have been significant initiatives in other areas of Armenian tourism development, given the short period of ten years during which Armenia has been working to re-establish the tourism industry.

Familiarization tours have been organized for foreign journalists, business people and tourism industry specialists. The private sector has cooperated to publish and disseminate tourism information and international television travel programmes have featured the attractions of Armenia. WTO and UNDP have been assisting in Armenia's tourism development and the government's Department of Tourism Development has taken several new initiatives to strengthen the integrity of the tourism industry overall, make a framework of related laws and regulations and set standards for tourism services.

Bangladesh

Globalization has contributed to recent general economic growth in Bangladesh, and it is assumed that the tourism sector has followed the general pattern. However, there has not yet been any assessment of the specific contribution of the tourism sector to gross domestic product (GDP). The two main components of tourism in Bangladesh consist of international tourists and domestic tourists. While data on income from domestic tourism has not been assessed, it was reported that arrivals of international tourists grew by an annual average of about 5 per cent from 1995 to 1999. Foreign exchange earnings from tourism grew by an annual average of 30 per cent during the same period. This shows that Bangladesh has an opportunity to gain benefits from international tourism.

Bangladesh prepared a Tourism Master Plan in 1991 with assistance from the United Nations Development Programme (UNDP) and the International Labour Organization (ILO), but resource constraints have prevented effective investment, marketing and promotion. A tourism policy was framed in 1992 and the government has started to plan and develop strategies. The National Tourism Council and an Advisory Committee on Tourism have been formed at the highest level, but an on-going sense of direction has yet to be formulated. Nevertheless, the government considers PASTA as an appropriate guideline and policy tool for balanced tourism development in Bangladesh.

In order to develop human resources, Bangladesh Parjatan Corporation (BPC) has responsibility for the state-operated tourism-training institute, the National

Hotel and tourism Training Institute (NHTTI). Since its establishment in 1974, NHTTI has been strengthened with assistance from UNDP and ILO.

There are a small number of private sector hotel and tourism schools, but they have limited resources and facilities. Some hotels have good in-service training and educational facilities. However, it is difficult to know if this meets human resource needs in the tourism sector. There has not been any systematic assessment of present and future human resource development requirements.

There is informal cooperation among institutes and NHTTI, but some time will be needed before establishing a national committee on human resources development in tourism. Bangladesh has not yet done any study on the economic impact of tourism.

However, general information shows tourism's economic significance according to its main features. Tourism is a labour-intensive industry with tourism facilities spread throughout the country. It contributes to growth in other related activities, such as restaurants, souvenir and handicraft shops, guide services and transportation services.

In Bangladesh, it is reported that a significant number of women have benefited from employment creation due to tourism. The government has taken the lead in creating a number of tourism facilities. However, the role of the private sector is being encouraged, especially to attract investment. The role of tourism is generally considered when formulating development programmes. Tourism is one of the thrust sectors for Bangladesh's industrial policy.

The government has been giving increased attention to preserving and developing the environment in relation to tourism development. Rules and guidelines for environmental management have been updated and strengthened in order to include environmental considerations in decision-making about any development activity.

Environmental impact analysis is now a prerequisite for planning and designing projects, whether they are new or involve modernizing existing facilities. There is a national committee headed by the prime minister to provide oversight on all environmental issues. Given the scale of tourism in Bangladesh and lack of overcrowding at tourist sites, the tourism sector is not seen as having any major negative impact on the environment. The government has taken a leading role in infrastructure development, including hotel accommodations.

A major constraint in Bangladesh's tourism industry is the limited number of hotels at standards expected by international tourists. Another constraint is an imbalance in the location of hotel accommodations; with most of them in Dhaka, while tourists seek accommodations in other parts of the country. The government has plans to establish tourist resorts, eco-parks and marine parks in order to more widely spread tourism facilities. The aim is to promote sustainable preservation of the biodiversity of Bangladesh's forests, coastal areas and islands. It is recognized that private investment is much needed to develop tourist facilities, and private investors have been showing increased interest.

There are now three international airports providing access to Bangladesh. The road system is being upgraded and extended in order to help encourage tourism. Improvements in ground transportation services have helped to overcome physical limits to accessibility. Health care facilities and emergency medical services are available in almost every part of the country. Immigration and customs regulations have been liberalized and simplified. BPC provides services to tourists through it information centers at a number of locations throughout the country. BPC has also published maps, brochures and guidebooks to assist tourists.

South Asian Association for Regional Cooperation (SAARC) has had a Technical Committee on Tourism since 1991, in which Bangladesh has been an active member. SAARC members have been considering various forms of cooperation in tourism development. When BIMST-EC (Bangladesh, India, Myanmar, Sri Lanka, Thailand-Economic Cooperation) was formed, tourism was identified as a major sector for subregional cooperation.

There have been meetings of BIMST-EC tourism experts in order to develop programmes and projects, including promotion of "Visit BIMST-EC Region" in 2001. Other significant initiatives in Bangladesh include giving three inter-ministerial committees oversight of tourism activities with a view to enhancing coordination. The three committees are: the National Tourism Council headed by the Prime Minister, the Advisory Committee headed by the minister in charge of tourism and the Coordination and Implementation Committee headed by the secretary of the Ministry of Tourism. These committees are considering the creation of an additional committee to be responsible for travel facilitation issues.

Cambodia

A specific tourism development policy in Cambodia was formulated within the overall First Socio-economic Development Plan (1996-2000). However, human resources development in the tourism sector has been severely constrained due to the low level of qualifications of tourism personnel in terms of average education level and low education standards. Tourism has expanded rapidly, and there has been fast-growing demand for more qualified personnel, especially people with foreign language capabilities. It was reported that the Ministry of Tourism had sufficient staff, but the need for training has been recognized. Strengthening human resources development within the Ministry of Tourism was considered to be a crucial first step in order for Cambodia to take other actions to develop human resources.

An economic impact analysis of tourism was conducted in 1995 under a tourism project of UNDP and WTO. However, there were few statistics and the accuracy was uncertain given the period of disruption to the national economy, followed by economic rehabilitation and very rapid economic change. As a result, there has been no detailed statistical analysis of the impact of tourism on the Cambodian economy in order to guide policy making.

The government has set forth the strategy for tourism development based on cultural heritage and the natural environment. Policies, planning and control measures for environmental management of tourism should focus on the carrying capacity of the environment; follow integrated land use planning for tourism areas; carefully manage visitor flows and use of national parks, wildlife sanctuaries and other protected sites; protect and manage forest resources in a sustainable way; and maintain environmental health and safety standards for residents and tourists. A public education campaign for residents and tourists was also considered as important to help control littering in public places. The tourism infrastructure at major cultural sites in Siem Reap province is being rehabilitated and reconstructed.

Urgent development was needed for all infrastructure components, particularly air transport, roads and water transportation services. Three priority locations for investment have been identified, investment incentives have been offered, investment laws and trade in services have been liberalized. In addition, Cambodia's Ministry of Tourism and the Tourism Authority of Thailand signed an Agreement on an Action Plan for Tourism Cooperation in 1998 covering three Cambodian provinces. Each province would have a master plan that included rehabilitation of tourism infrastructure. The role of the private sector in tourism development has been recognized as important. Coordination among private enterprises in the tourism sector was encouraged along with cooperation between the public and private sectors. Some requirements related to travel facilitation have been liberalized by allowing visas on arrival and border passes. Four international checkpoints have been designated for entry by land, and one can issue visas on arrival. There are two international checkpoints for arrivals by air.

The Ministry of Tourism is active in ASEAN tourism cooperation and has signed bilateral tourism cooperation agreements with four other ASEAN members, as well as China. There are bilateral memoranda on tourism cooperation with India and Indonesia, and plans to sign with the Philippines and Brunei Darussalam. At the subregional level, Cambodia participates actively in the Working Group on the Greater Mekong Subregion Tourism Sector. One new initiative by the Ministry of Tourism has encouraged the formation of tourism industry associations since 1996. This is related to the general policy of encouraging private sector participation by providing forums for discussing issues of common interest and encouraging the private sector to be self-regulating.

China

The unique natural endowments, long history, diverse cultural heritage of various ethnic groups and tradition of hospitality form the basis for tourism development in China. Rational use of resources to develop tourism was considered as important for national economic development to improve people's living standards in ways that would be sustainable and carry forward national and cultural traditions. In terms of human resources development, the government considers that tourism managers, tourists and the public needed enhanced awareness and more scientific knowledge about sustainable tourism development.

China has a seven-point strategy as a basic framework for sustainable tourism development that seeks to balance rational use of resources for positive economic impact with environmental protection. One point of the strategy emphasizes giving full play to market mechanisms and promoting the government's role in establishment of a cooperative institutional safeguard system. This would help at the macroeconomic level by replacing some traditional industries that used resources inefficiently and caused pollution.

Environmental protection and scientific management as key parts of a strategy of sustainable tourism development was the fundamental state policy of the National Tourism Development Plan, 1996-2000. Scientific management of natural and cultural resources would involve active development of ecotourism, especially for protecting biodiversity.

China has strengthened its legal and technical standards in order to protect tourism resources. Since the 1980s, this has included the Law on Environmental Protection, Rules and Regulations on National Scenic Spots and Regulations on Forests and Parks. At the same time, it was recognized that investors were one of several groups of stakeholders, and meeting everyone's interests required integrated coordination and management of the whole industry.

Science and technology could also help to build institutional and infrastructural safeguards for sustainable tourism development. The government has identified 500 cultural relics protection sites at the national level, 99 cities of historical and cultural renown and 119 scenic spots at the national level. More than 700 nature conservation zones have been established, as well as more than 120 national and provincial holiday resorts.

Enhancing international cooperation was considered integral to promoting sustainable tourism development based on equal participation by all countries. Countries should formulate plans that are relevant to national conditions, but they should also be aware of any negative impact on neighbouring countries. International cooperation would facilitate sharing resources and technology and help developing countries to build their capacities for sustainable tourism development.

The National Tourism Administration of China has proposed guidelines on promoting tourism development at the Sixth Annual Session of the Parliamentarian Congress on Environment and Development in Asia and the Pacific. China has also emphasized public awareness and education campaigns on sustainable tourism development, and there have been pilot projects involving ecotourism. One initiative under China's seven-point strategic policy for tourism development involves setting up model ecotourism projects. An important part of ecotourism projects involves action to preserve and maintain the continuity of the cultural heritage.

Hong Kong, China

The tourism industry is one of the most important sources of foreign exchange earnings for Hong Kong, China. The tourism vision follows from the industry's economic importance, increased regional competition and the need to continually upgrade the overall tourism product to meet future challenges. Hong Kong, China would be promoted as Asia's premier international city for leisure and business visitors. This includes a focus on human resources development to improve standards and performance.

Emphasis is on professionalism and promoting a hospitality culture, as well as ensuring an adequate supply of skilled personnel through liaison with industry bodies. The tourism industry contributed over 4 per cent to GDP in 1999. The number of visitors has been growing since 1998, but tourism still needed proper recognition as a major sector of the economy. The Tourism Development Action Programme would help since it included at least two major new projects, a number of small-scale projects and a Rapid Enhancement Programme that focused on improvements to existing popular locations.

Hong Kong, China has been giving greater attention to preserving and restoring its historical and archeological heritage and making this part of the tourist attractions. The country parks, woodland trails and less urbanized island locations have been receiving greater attention, as they become more popular with tourists. About 40 per cent of the land area is country parks. The Commerce and Industry Bureau has reported that a systematic approach would be needed when opening countryside areas to tourism. Current international trends involving ecotourism and cultural-heritage tourism will be the focus of future tourism development.

Additional infrastructure is considered as essential to fulfill the vision of becoming a world city of Asia. At least four major infrastructure developments have been envisioned and their feasibility will be studied. These include a new cruise terminal, a full-scale convention and exhibition center, a performing arts venue and a multi-purpose stadium. Domestic and foreign expertise and investment has been welcomed, including open international competition to design and develop an international performing arts centre to be linked to other infrastructure development.

Most aspects of travel facilitation have been eased in order to make the visa regime a benchmark providing a competitive advantage. Visitors from Taiwan Province of China now experience simpler electronic processing arrangements, and a group tour scheme for visitors from mainland China has been expanded. On-going cooperation with authorities in Beijing has helped simplify procedures for business visitors.

Myanmar

Tourism has become a growth sector since policies were liberalized to create a market-oriented economy. The Myanmar Tourism Law of 1990 was revised in 1993 to promote systematic development and encourage private sector participation. Myanmar observed that the demand for personnel trained to international standards has been strong since 1992. The Ministry of Hotels and Tourism conducts training programmes and courses and also collaborates with the Network of Asia-Pacific Education and Training Institutes in Tourism (APETIT), ESCAP, the World Tourism Organization (WTO), the Mekong Institute, ASEAN and others, such as the Singapore Tourism Board and the Tourism Authority of Thailand.

Myanmar reported that liberalized entry formalities and the 1996 launch of "Visit Myanmar Year" had caused a major increase in tourism arrivals, although the total number of visitors had already peaked at about 200,000 per year. The largest share of tourists has been from Asian countries. No information has been reported on whether a systematic economic impact assessment has been done. Myanmar reported that tourism was being developed in close cooperation with other ministries to ensure conservation of the natural environment and preservation of the cultural heritage. Relevant government agencies have worked with UNESCO to preserve an archaeological zone at Bagan. Conservation through forest management involves a protective area system.

Myanmar reported on the importance of infrastructure for the future of the tourism industry with an emphasis on establishing regular flights, especially long-haul flights that could use the new international airport at Mandalay. Road networks would also be expanded. A number of cruise ships called at Yangon port and cruise tourists are able to make linkages with special excursions by chartered flights to inland tourist destinations. Foreign investment, which has concentrated mostly on hotel projects in the major cities, plus a few at border areas and beaches, has been affected by the Asian financial crisis.

Myanmar has relaxed some visa requirements in order to facilitate travel. Charter flights, cruises and certain other group tours may be granted visa on arrival based on prior arrangement with the Ministry of Hotels and Tourism. Tourists from ASEAN member countries who have diplomatic and official passports are allowed visa free entry. Only a few embassies of Myanmar are able to issue entry visas by email or through the Internet. Entry overland at borders with neighbouring countries has been made easier for some categories of tourists who are issued border passes. Tourists with border passes who come through the border between Myanmar and Thailand are allowed to travel as far as Yangon if they have prior permission.

Myanmar participates in the Working Group on the Greater Mekong Subregion Tourism Sector, BIMST-EC and ASEAN. At the same time, Myanmar has bilateral tourism mutual cooperation agreements with the other five countries of the Greater Mekong subregion. Among other related initiatives, Myanmar reported that it supported development of a campaign initiated by Thailand for cultural tour packages known as "Great Wonders of Suvana Phumi" involving four countries of the Greater Mekong subregion.

At the national level, the Tourism Development Management Committee was formed to encourage high-level coordination within the government and include private sector participation as well. There is still a lack of awareness about Myanmar as a tourist destination, due in part to the low profile of tourism for about 30 years. The potential for tourism development in Myanmar must face with constraints caused by inadequate infrastructure and lack of funds for promotion worldwide using modern information technology. The government has committed itself to balanced tourism development that retains the cultural heritage while developing infrastructure in line with the social and economic capacity to absorb tourism growth.

Philippines

Tourism has been one of the top foreign exchange earners for the Philippine economy, accounting for 8.7 per cent of GDP in 1997. At the same time, tourism has been important for direct employment creation, as well as indirect employment in many other sectors. Training programmes for frontline tourism services organized by the Department of Tourism (DOT) have become institutionalized at the national and local levels. DOT has organized specialized training programmes focused on sustainable tourism and environmental awareness. The Philippines' DOT has been developing tourism satellite accounting (TSA) in cooperation with the National Economic Development Authority and National Statistics Office based on WTO and the World Travel and Tourism Council (WTTC) methodology. Once TSA is completed, stakeholders at the national and local levels would be invited to workshops and seminars in order to share the information about the socio-economic impact of tourism in the Philippines.

The Philippines reported on several initiatives involving sustainable tourism aimed at protecting the environment, preserving cultural heritage and promoting community involvement. Green Globe action plans have been made for two pilot areas. An executive order by the President in 1999 established guidelines for ecotourism and created a National Ecotourism Development Council to make policy along with structures to review and approve ecotourism projects. In October 1999, a National Ecotourism Congress was organized to help formulate the national ecotourism policy. At the community level, whale-watching tourism programs have been organized based on coordination with other agencies and NGOs in order to provide supplemental livelihoods for local communities.

The Philippines has completed national and regional tourism master plans to identify priority tourism development for local and foreign investment. The plans should ensure orderly and sustainable use of natural and cultural resources and extensive consultation with various stakeholders. Tourism projects are subject to the Investment Priorities Plan of the DOT. In 1999, DOT endorsed 143 tourism projects for incentives under the Investment Priorities Plan. Government measures to stimulate tourism investments are contained in three general acts and plans, which cover tourism and infrastructure. The Build-Operate-Transfer Act encourages the private sector to develop infrastructure. The Foreign Investment Act of 1991 and its amendments allow 100 per cent foreign equity participation in almost all tourism projects.

An economic mobilization group (EMG) was established in 1999 to resolve some opposing viewpoints in the government about travel facilitation. The EMG is comprised of government agencies, legislators and private sector representatives. Immigration and customs officials have started working towards greater coordination to facilitate procedures at international airports and seaports. A clear process and guidelines are being formulated to liberalize aviation policy. Safety standards and related measures are disseminated through the media and foreign embassies to inform international tourists.

The Philippines has been actively involved in ASEAN, BIMP-EAGA and APEC. The Philippines advocated that there should be greater cooperation among APEC members to promote sustainable tourism. The Philippines has been participating in many conferences and meetings to share experiences with best practices and lessons learned about sustainable tourism development. The Philippines' emphasis on sustainable tourism is also pursued through bilateral and multilateral cooperation, including cooperation with the Government of New Zealand to formulate a National Ecotourism Strategy.

The Philippines reported on several projects that were initiated in support of the PASTA strategies. One initiative aims to institutionalize the National Ecotourism Development Council, National Ecotourism Steering Committee and the Regional Ecotourism Committees to work on the National Ecotourism Strategy. A related initiative would formulate accreditation programmes on HRD for ecotourism. Action to promote community-based tourism includes agri-tourism and coastal resource management for sustainable tourism. The Sustainable Environment Management Program for Northern Palawan has financial assistance from the Japan Bank for International Cooperation to develop environment critical area network zoning and provide soil erosion protection and project management, as well as sustainable tourism development.

Republic of Korea

In view of many technological changes, rising levels of income and increased leisure time for many people worldwide, tourism is expected to be a strategic force for socio-economic development. The Republic of Korea intends actively promote tourism to gain benefits from the global trends in the tourism industry. Within the Korean tourism sector, there is a need for more professional human resources management as a crucial component for sustaining tourism development.

A variety of training and education programmes have expanded steadily, along with the number of institutions doing research and training. The government has had a personnel qualification system covering jobs in the tourist industry. Two universities are already members of APETIT, and more are expected to join.

The Republic of Korea stated that the economic impact of tourism has already been studied, but data and findings now need to be updated. This would give a better picture of the appropriate economic role of tourism. At the same time, there have been policies aimed at strategic marketing and large-scale development of tourism.

The Republic of Korea also seeks to build a sense of tourism ethics and work towards making tourism a knowledge-based industry that creates friendship and prosperity throughout the Asian and Pacific region. The Ministry of Culture and Tourism of the Government of the Republic of Korea has planned to work closely with the Ministry of Environment in order to utilize eco-system preservation areas as ecotourism resources to be protected and preserved as unique to the country.

A significant part of the government budget in the Republic of Korea would be devoted to expanding tourism infrastructure to promote tourism in the twenty-first century. Research is being done on the creation of new, large-scale tourism projects, such as the South Coast Tour Belt, Confucian Culture Zone in Northern Kyongbuk area and a development project to link Mt. Sorak to Mt. Keumgang with a view to future increases in South-North tourism exchanges. The Government of the Republic of Korea has taken measures to relax over 60 rules and regulations to facilitate travel and improve the tourist information system for both domestic and international tourists. Tourism information centers have been established in Seoul, Kwangju and other major cities. City and tourist maps have also been printed.

In July 2000, the Republic of Korea held the first APEC Meeting of Ministers Responsible for Tourism, which was attended by tourism officials from 21 APEC-member countries. The Seoul Declaration affirmed APEC-member countries' goal to develop and enhance the contribution of tourism to the region by removing impediments, increasing access, managing tourism to be sustainable and recognizing tourism as an engine for development. Since the Republic of Korea considers tourism as a strategic force for world development in the twenty-first century, it has developed "Tourism Vision 21" as a five-year plan (1999-2003) and declared 2001 as "Visit Korea Year". This includes plans for the growth of tourism expected in the twenty-first century due to globalization and information technology.

American Samoa

The tourism sector has had an overall positive impact on socio-economic development and the rate of growth has been increasing progressively. A tourism development plan is clearly needed in American Samoa in order to help tourism reach its full potential. The government and the private sector have been working together to design such a plan. However, the local legislature has not yet passed the plan. Human resources development for the tourism sector consists of off-island training and training at the American Samoa Community College (ASCC).

By summer 2001, a tourism industry management course will be offered at ASCC. Off-island training has included training through the EDIT University of Hawaii-Manoa campus, seminars in environmental tourism awareness as part of the South Pacific Regional Environmental Programme; and workshops and training with the South Pacific Tourism Organization along with regional seminars for staff development.

The economic development of tourism in American Samoa has involved the development of bed and breakfast accommodations in various parts of the island, a recreational diving club set up by local divers and production of handicrafts by youths and senior citizens. Ecotourism has been developed through the establishment of American Samoa National Park. A sports stadium and the hosting of the 1997 South Pacific Mini Games has helped increase the impact of sports tourism.

Environmental management of tourism places emphasis on the Samoan culture and lifestyle through community and village-based tourism as a way to protect and sustain the island environment. The national park provides an area for learning about how to conserve nature and the cultural heritage. Most infrastructure development in American Samoa in recent years has been concentrated in the area around the airport. The runway has been lengthened and expanded and the airport terminal has been renovated.

A new hotel with 100 rooms, full conference facilities and a restaurant has been approved for development and will involve some foreign investment. One existing hotel built in the mid-1960s may be sold in order to overcome the lack of maintenance that has limited the tourism potential. The overall aim is to promote the island and attract more tourists. Action to facilitate travel has included a workshop for immigration officials to address a number of current issues and the laws involving both American Samoa and (formerly Western) Samoa. Ongoing high-level executive meetings are also held between officials to help promote tourism development for both sets of islands.

The South Pacific Tourism Organization provides the regional forum for American Samoa to join in promotional and educational activities, including workshops and seminars. Officials from American Samoa attend the tourism convention organized in Samoa. One major initiative is a memorandum of understanding between American Samoa and (formerly Western) Samoa to jointly promote South Pacific Island Samoa as a package for international tourists. American Samoa has hosted or participated in a number of special subregional events that contribute to tourism development.

Sri Lanka

Tourism in Sri Lanka is considered as an industry driven by the private sector with active support by the public sector. Tourism makes a major contribution to GDP, creates a significant number of jobs and earns a considerable share of foreign exchange. Social and economic development in various parts of the country, especially semi-urban and rural areas, is enhanced by the tourism sector. At the community level there is self-employment in producing and selling handicrafts and food. Food and agricultural products are sold to hotels and restaurants, and self-employed people can provide transport for tourists.

Sri Lanka places strong emphasis on human resources development in order to provide high quality tourism services. A modern hotel school has been established to provide a wide range of training and special programmes at the national level and there are plans to have exchanges with other countries in the region. Provinces would be able to set up satellite schools to meet local needs and help unemployed youth. The Ceylon Tourist Board also conducts special training programmes. The private sector is also encouraged and supported by the government to provide tourism training.

By 1999 there were about 436,000 tourist arrivals and tourism earned about US$ 281 million. Tourism was also declared a thrust industry in 1999 in view of its economic contribution, the increased role of the private sector and its attractiveness for foreign investors. By 2000, tourism was the fourth largest source of foreign exchange earnings. The government receives income from tourism through direct and indirect taxes. Several government agencies can earn income from tourism through admission fees collected at archeological sites, nature parks, national parks, zoological gardens and museum. Within the government, the Ministry of Tourism and Civil Aviation has been working closely with the Ceylon Tourist Board and the Ceylon Hotels Corporation in tourism planning.

Sri Lanka has a long history of environmental management based on traditional village structures that conserve and protect the forest and water sources. At present, specific government agencies are responsible for preserving and protecting the natural environment and for managing and preserving heritage sites. There is a Central Environmental Authority advised by an Environmental Council that involves the Ministry of Tourism and Civil Aviation. Formal environmental impact assessments are required for hotel projects approved by the Ceylon Tourist Board. Ecotourism is new for Sri Lanka, but the need for clear policy guidelines has been recognized. Important infrastructure issues arise from the fact that tourism tended to be seasonal and concentrated in a few resorts in Sri Lanka. In order to upgrade and modernize facilities and infrastructure, the government has sought assistance from UNDP for a ten-year comprehensive infrastructure development programme.

Thailand

The travel and tourism industry in Thailand had survived the economic crisis of 1997 remarkably well and reported a record number of tourist arrivals and increased earnings from tourism. However, the continued growth in international tourist arrivals has created challenges for human resources development in terms of education and training, skill requirements and opportunities for job advancement. The demand for labour in the tourism sector was expected to increase by 56 per cent per year, with the greatest demand in the accommodation and restaurant business. At the same time, just over half of all people working in the tourism industry were educated only to the high school level. Many of these people had few opportunities for training, especially to develop technical skills and management and language capability.

General data suggests that tourism has become quite important for the Thai economy. It accounted for 4.8 per cent of GDP in 1999 and tourism has been projected to grow by an average of 6.5 per cent a year from 1999 to 2010. Tourism accounted for about 11 per cent of total employment in 1999. In order to gain reliable data about the economic impact of tourism, the Thai government has approved a budget to develop a tourism satellite account

(TSA). The Tourism Authority of Thailand (TAT) has been working closely with WTO and WTTC since 1997 to develop a TSA. Once it is developed, TSA would be used to propose a national tourism policy. The National Economic and Social Development Board (NESDB) and National Statistical Office have also been working on the TSA project.

Thailand recognized that management of tourism resources should involve people at all levels in the industry. All stakeholders have a role in monitoring the impact of tourism, assessing the environment, collecting data and balancing carrying capacity with tourists' demand. Strong emphasis is given to ecological and cultural sensitivity, conserving biodiversity, finding alternative energy sources and managing waste disposal. The government would have a major role through linkages between policy and community participation, as well as developing national laws and regulations.

In Thailand, infrastructure development and investment policies would encourage the private sector to accelerate tourism investment and spread development to rural areas. A committee in each province would prepare tourism investment plans to inform investors. It is expected that these would be part of each province's economic strategic plan to cover agriculture, industry and services. However, systematic criteria and comparative data were still needed.

A communication network would make tourism development more convenient, including plans for road, railway and airline networks to neighbouring countries. Thailand had received a tourism development and promotion loan from the Overseas Economic Cooperation Fund of Japan (OECF), which targeted eight provinces in the North, North-East and South for phase 2. Several ministries have projects under the loan, plus TAT and private consultants to provide management and coordination.

Thailand had few impediments related to visas for international tourists, especially from major markets. Facilitation of travel in the form of visa exemptions or visa on arrival applies to about 158 countries. Immigration procedures have been facilitated for tourists at 30 permanent checkpoints and other checkpoints could be opened on request. Slow immigration procedures when the inflow of tourists becomes congested, particularly at the main international airport was one obstacle.

Thailand is active in subregional cooperation by promoting tourism in the Greater Mekong Subregion (GMS) as important for the overall development of all countries in the Working Group on the GMS Tourism Sector. TAT serves as coordinator for tourism projects through the Agency for Coordinating Mekong Tourism Activities (AMTA). Coordination under AMTA has involved subregional marketing activities and cooperation in human resources development.

TAT has taken a new initiative by developing the Focus Group as a tool for adjusting the tourism plan. The Focus Group would establish cooperation among airlines and entrepreneurs to help evaluate and adjust the tourism plan through participatory management that would create benefits for the whole industry. The Thai government has taken another major initiative to provide a budget that would allow TAT to develop the TSA within a period of five years in order to propose a national policy on tourism.

Turkey

Recent growth of the tourism industry in Turkey has followed the global pattern of rapid expansion in line with rising standards of living, increased leisure time for travel and improved infrastructure. The tourism industry in Turkey contributes significantly to foreign exchange earnings and employment. In view of its economic importance, the Turkish Tourism Policy seeks more efficiency in the sector and the government gives priority to training qualified personnel. Most activities to develop human resources are carried out by the private sector. However, the government provides vocational training. The Turkish Tourism Policy aims to extend the economic benefits from tourism to the people, while ensuring that tourism policies are environmentally sound and sustainable.

Tourism is primarily a private sector industry, but tourism facilities must be licensed either by municipalities or the Ministry of Tourism. Such licensing by the Ministry is intended to guarantee that the quality of services conform to international standards. The tourism industry has been undergoing dynamic change recently, so effective support and incentives would be needed from the government. In addition, the government is responsible for research and statistics to help evaluate the impact of tourism. One principle of the Turkish Tourism Policy is to ensure the continuity of natural and cultural assets, which means giving priority to environmental protection and the cultural heritage. The government has the main responsibility for environmental protection.

Turkey has a number of environmental management projects, such as the Mediterranean and Aegean Coastline

Tourism Infrastructure Management Project and the Blue Flag Campaign to ensure water quality. There is also a master plan for yacht tourism. The Government of Turkey is responsible for infrastructure and public services, although incentives are granted under the Tourism Encouragement Law. The Ministry of Tourism provides the overall orientation and coordination. However, publicly owned tourism establishments will be gradually privatized. Foreign investment in the tourism sector is encouraged according to Foreign Investment Law number 6224.

The Yacht Tourism Master Plan is intended to encourage yacht tourism and overcome legislative bottlenecks since Turkey has a comparative advantage in attracting this form of tourism. Berthing capacity for yachts would be increased. The geographic diversity and rich cultural heritage provide a broad range of alternative tourism experiences. The Ministry of Tourism has been working to revitalize the Silk Road and restoring eleven caravan serais with the help of private investors using the build-operate-transfer model. Plans by the Ministry of Tourism of Turkey to develop tourism along the Silk Road would involve cooperation to ensure that it becomes a route of international peace and fraternity. Turkey reported that the Foundation for Environmental Education in Europe helped to design the Blue Flag Campaign in order to keep lake and seawater clean and improve the quality of services at beaches and marinas.

Uzbekistan

Tourism development aimed at global markets has a relatively short history starting in 1989 and becoming more important since 1991, when Uzbekistan became an independent republic. In the years immediately after independence, tourism numbers declined. However, the efforts of Uzbektourism and Uzbekistan Airways built up marketing and direct access to principal tourist markets in Germany, France and the United Kingdom. There has also been success in strengthening the tourism potential in secondary markets, such as Italy, the Netherlands, Japan, Republic of Korea, the United States and Russia.

The main challenge is creating greater international awareness for tourism in Uzbekistan. At the same time, there are a number of related challenges or problems that need to be addressed within the Uzbek tourism industry concerning human resources development, the capabilities of the NTO (Uzbektourism), environmental management, tourism infrastructure and investment, travel facilitation and the government's overall tourism development strategy. A tourism development and marketing action plan has been proposed for Uzbekistan and covers the challenges listed above. The general aim of the action plan would be to establish Uzbekistan as the "Crossroads of the Great Silk Road".

In terms of human resources development, the action plan identified management training as the focus with priority given to the hotel sector, heritage sites and the NTO. Given the situation in the Uzbek tourism industry, the action plan advocated a top-down approach where 100 top managers in key positions would be trained first so that they, in turn, could become trainers in their organizations. It was expected that this would create a cascading effect throughout the industry. Other priorities for human resources development include establishing a hotel and catering school of international standard, training of personnel working at the airport and Uzbekistan Airways and training of NTO personnel in other countries.

The economic impact of tourism in Uzbekistan derives from two distinct types of tourists: international tourists arriving by air on long-haul flights and "day" tourists from neighbouring Central Asian countries. According to Uzbektourism, the total number of foreign visitors in 1996 was 174,000 and tourism revenue amounted to about US$ 198 million. It was projected that there would be about 650,000 visitors in 2000 with revenue of about US$ 1 billion. The main destinations for most tourists have been the cities of Samarkand, Bukhara and Khiva with an emphasis on the cultural and historical heritage. The average length of stay has been 6 to 9 nights. Challenges for the economic development of tourism would be to spread the impact, increase the length of stay and attract other tourist market segments with an interest in skiing, trekking, archeology and ecology.

The environmental management of tourism is expected to become a more important issue area for Uzbekistan, especially if there are more tourists visiting heritage sites and there is an expansion of tourist activities to include ecotourism and outdoor sports. A number of recommendations for tourism development have focused on environmental and cultural attractions, including Zamir National Park, scenic tours between the main tourist destinations, short stays with families in typical Uzbek villages and promoting nature and cultural attractions of the Ferghana Valley. Trekking and camping holidays in the Zarafshan Mountains are also being considered.

Infrastructure development for tourism development has focused mostly on upgrading and modernizing existing facilities, especially the main airports, hotels and ground transport equipment.Uzbekistan can be considered as an economy in transition where the roles of the public sector and private sectors need careful planning for future sustainable tourism development. In this issue area the role of Uzbektourism has to be given special consideration.

At present, Uzektourism is involved in hotel and tour management as well as tourism promotion and acting as the NTO. It could be useful to study the experience of other countries where hotel and tour management and tourism advertising, marketing and promotion might be taken over by the private sector given the costs involved. One possible constraint observed in Uzbekistan is that the privatization began only in 1994. There has been progress in attracting foreign investment and an action programme for sustainable tourism development should help direct foreign investors to the tourism sector. At the same time, the institutional framework for tourism could also be analyzed as part of infrastructure development. Along these lines, the government has proposed to establish a new Department of Culture, Tourism and Sports. Promoting public-private sector partnerships, especially through encouragement to small and medium-sized enterprises (SMEs), could help support tourism marketing and promotion in international markets.

Facilitation of travel to Uzbekistan involves issues related to political stability in the Central Asian region and media reports that create negative images. At the same time, other facilitation issues include the cumbersome visa formalities, the use of parallel exchange rates and various limitations to locations and sites of tourism interest. If tourism is expected to have a significant role in economic development, then issues of facilitation require careful assessment by the government in terms of how open the country can be to international tourism. At the same time, more practical aspects of facilitation also need to be addressed, such as road maps and sign posting that meet international standards and greater choices for travelers in terms of package tours and accommodations in various price ranges.

The main focus of regional cooperation and new initiatives by Uzbekistan is the Silk Road. In order to develop tourism and market the country in major tourist source countries, Uzbekistan has the advantage of being a strategic cross roads between Europe and Asia along the historical Silk Road. There is generally good road infrastructure within the country and the Silk Road can be the attraction for visits to multiple destinations involving several countries in the region. The annual Tashkent International Tourism Fair is one possible venue for workshops with tour operators to create greater awareness of Uzbekistan, its cultural heritage, the natural environment and the Silk Road. Overall, the development of sustainable tourism in Uzbekistan would require new policies in the possible form of an action plan, new institutional structures, incentives for private sector investment and training of human resources.

Actions taken by Organizations

According to PASTA, international and regional organizations would be taking supporting actions in the six theme areas. Reports by twelve organizations show that there is strong support for regional and subregional cooperation with an emphasis on sharing information, experiences, facilities and expertise. Action by international and regional organizations can help create opportunities for greater access, provide resources and help strengthen capabilities and encourage arrangements that focus on sustainability in tourism development. The activities of international and regional organizations in the Asian and Pacific region can promote sustainable tourism development by conserving scarce resources, promoting cultural and economic understanding, increasing the frequency of international contacts and exchanges and reducing unnecessary competition.

Asian Development Bank

The Asian Development Bank (ADB) supports subregional cooperation in combination with human resources development and infrastructure development through its regional technical assistance to the Greater Mekong Subregional Cooperation (GMS). The overall objective is to help strengthen economic and social well-being in the six countries of the region. Tourism development was identified as a priority initiative and the Working Group of the GMS Tourism Sector was formed in 1995 through joint efforts of ESCAP and ADB. The Working Group is comprised of NTOs of the six countries and provides guidance and support for implementation of priority projects. By 1997, the secretariat of the Working Group was formed as the Agency for Coordinating Mekong Tourism Activities (AMTA) under the responsibility of the Tourism Authority of Thailand.

Most support activities of ADB are in the form of regional technical assistance to address a number of subregional tourism issues. Since 1995 there has been regional technical assistance to train trainers in tourism, make a comprehensive assessment of the feasibility of tourism development along the Mekong River, develop training for tourism planning and management, identify and evaluate the feasibility of priority tourism infrastructure development. ADB cooperates with a number of other regional and international organizations to promote increased tourism in the GMS as a strategy to help alleviate poverty, develop human resources and contribute to sustainable development along the Mekong River.

The ADB has identified inadequate infrastructure as the principal constraint to tourism development in the GMS and focuses technical assistance on identifying priority tourism infrastructure needs and promoting related mechanisms that can strengthen cooperation among the six countries along the Mekong River. ADB also provides technical assistance at the national level in order to strengthen tourism planning, infrastructure development and ecotourism as part of overall environmental management of tourism. Emphasis is on the social and environmental impact of tourism and the need to include all stakeholders when planning and designing projects with ADB assistance.

Asia-Pacific Economic Cooperation Secretariat

The Asia-Pacific Economic Cooperation Secretariat (APEC) organized an APEC Tourism Working Group (TWG) that has been sharing information, exchanging views and developing areas of cooperation since 1991. TWG has three areas of work in its programme:

(1) trade and investment liberalization,

(2) facilitation and

(3) economic and technical cooperation.

Priority has recently focused on collective actions to overcome impediments to tourism growth.

A comprehensive inventory of barriers to travel in the APEC region has been compiled. APEC members have also agreed to a series of collective actions that address impediments to tourism growth. A comprehensive analysis of the economic impact of travel and tourism in the APEC region with forecasts to 2010 was published by the TWG in cooperation with WTTC. The First APEC Tourism Forum was held in April 2000 at Hong Kong, China in order to promote private sector participation in cooperation with WTTC, the Pacific Asia Travel Association (PATA) and WTO.

Since 1999, APEC members and the TWG have developed the APEC Tourism Charter that would serve as a statement of ministerial purposes and intent to achieve four policy goals:

(1) remove impediments to tourism business and investment,

(2) increase mobility of visitors and tourism demand in the APEC region,

(3) manage tourism in ways that are sustainable and

(4) recognize tourism as a vehicle for socio-economic development.

At the First Ministerial Meeting of Ministers Responsible for Tourism in July 2000, the Seoul Declaration on an APEC Tourism Charter was adopted. The TWG would be responsible for compiling individual and collective action plans to achieve the four policy goals. Other parts of the work programme of the TWG include promotion of tourism as a means to achieve sustainable economic development with a focus on best practices; human resources development with skills standardization; information exchange to enhance public-private sector cooperation; and promotion of links with other APEC working groups relevant to the tourism industry.

Indian Ocean Tourism Organisation

The Indian Ocean Tourism Organisation (IOTO) supports its member countries based on the vision of having every destination in the region optimize its tourism potential based on sustainable approaches for the benefit of the people. Much of IOTO work focuses on tourism activities that relate to its coastal tourism initiative. Besides a set of principles for coastal zone management (CZM) and tourism based on integrated national planning and sound environmental management of tourism, there is a five-point action programme for sustainable tourism in coastal environments of the Indian Ocean region. It was compiled during a recent workshop held at Kuala Lumpur. The five points of the action programme for sustainable tourism in coastal environments of the Indian Ocean region include:

(1) creating a tourism resource center with guidelines for CZM;

(2) setting up an advisory group with teams of experts to advise decision-makers, tourism developers, operators and local communities;

(3) starting educational pilot projects aimed at having operational staff participate actively in sustainable tourism development and environmental protection;

(4) introducing eco-labels to have international certification of coastal tourism operations with related workshops for evaluation and monitoring; and

(5) actively supporting initiatives for involving local communities and staff in sustainable tourism development.

In addition to making local communities aware of being stakeholders, the action programme would be developed and implemented jointly with local NGOs. Furthermore, involving local communities, resort operators, employees and guests in costal tourism management would ensure that the environment is appreciated and protected as much as the benefits of investment and the jobs created. All stakeholders would be more aware of the dangers of over use and value environmental management.

International Civil Aviation Organization Asia and Pacific Office

The International Civil Aviation Organization Asia and Pacific Office (ICAO) takes a number of actions aimed at facilitating travel worldwide and in the region. One concerns the role air transportation in promoting tourism, where ICAO focuses on streamlining facilitation systems and procedures as well as enhancing flight safety and security. Systems and procedures have become more efficient as countries introduce machine-readable passports and visas developed by ICAO. Flight safety and aviation security oversight programmes have been initiated in some countries and more are planned. In relation to tourism development, the work of ICAO aims to help the Asian and Pacific region create destinations that are attractive, accessible, safe and secure.

International Labour Office

The work of the International Labour Office (ILO) focuses on human resources development in the hotel, catering and tourism sectors. ILO held its tripartite meeting from 2 to 6 April 2001. A background report, "Human Resources Development, Employment and Globalization in the Hotel, Catering and Tourism Sector", was prepared as an input. The ILO would contribute to work being done on Tourism Satellite Accounts by extending the coverage to tourism labour statistics. The ILO background report showed the employment significance of the tourism industry.

Direct or "face-to-face" services to tourists represented between 3 and 4 per cent of GDP in most of the world economy and employed about 3 per cent of the world's total labour force. With the addition of industries that serve tourists indirectly by providing infrastructure or inputs to the direct tourism industry, the total tourism-related economy has been estimated by WTTC to produce as much as 11 per cent of GDP and to employ 8 per cent of the labour force worldwide. Worldwide, one job in the direct tourism industry induces about one-and-a-half additional (indirect) jobs in the tourism-related economy.

The ILO background paper described the main human resource features of enterprises in the tourism sector. Most usually employed only a small core of permanent and full-time staff. Other staff were employed with part-time, seasonal and casual labour arrangements. Up to half the workers in the industry were under 25 years old and up to 70 per cent were women. Staff turnover has been a serious issue, and employers often had to find new staff for up to half or more of their posts every year. Unattractive working conditions were not the only reason for high turnover. Other reasons for employee turnover included: poor career prospects, low pay, unsocial working hours and physical stress.

There are several other issues of concern to ILO and the tripartite partners. With the growth in nature tourism, rural, agri- or ecotourism and adventure tourism, people in remote areas could benefit from employment and income generated by tourism. However, ensuring that the benefits exceed the potential damage would need the proper involvement of local populations and regulation in order to reduce or prevent unfair competition. Sustainable development of these tourism forms therefore requires participatory institutions and social dialogue in communities.

Another human resources issue concerns very young children who work in all kinds of tourism-related occupations. The worst form of child labour in tourism is in sex tourism, and the international community has expressed concern and formed a task force against the commercial sexual exploitation of children to promote appropriate counter-measures. The industry also has developed innovative programmes to prevent and combat child prostitution in tourism.

New customer demands, new technologies, intense competition and continuing shortages of job applicants show that human resources development issues need much more attention. New forms of work organization are increasingly important factors for boosting productivity. At the same time, more tourism occupations demand higher skills, especially among managers and staff in direct contact with customers.

The ILO Tripartite Meeting had four main topics for discussion:

(1) globalization,

(2) employment creation and working conditions,

(3) human resources development and

(4) social dialogue.

Detailed issues under these topics included, among others: measures that could be taken to enhance the employment of women in the tourism sector; obstacles to the ratification and implementation of the Working Conditions (Hotels and Restaurants) Convention, 1991 (No. 172), and what measures should be taken to promote ratification; strategies for human resources development to ensure that workers are attracted to and retained; measures to be taken to increase training opportunities for workers in small and medium-sized enterprises; and how to enhance vocational training, particularly in developing countries.

Pacific Asia Travel Association

The Pacific Asia Travel Association (PATA) is firmly committed to both the ideal of sustainable tourism and its practice in the day-to-day operations of the tourism industry. Accordingly PATA would be:

(1) Adopting and promoting the PATA Code of Environmental Conduct and its application in the industry;

(2) Committing to working with partner organizations in the public and private sectors;

(3) Conducting meetings and workshops to raise the level of awareness about the elements behind sustainable tourism; and

(4) Identifying and widely disseminating experiences with best practices.

These elements were reaffirmed at PATA's Fiftieth Annual Conference, held in April 2001, in a specific resolution aimed at a vision for the next fifty years of PATA and its role in promoting responsible and sustainable tourism in the Asian and Pacific region.

Tumen Secretariat

The Tumen Secretariat works in association with UNDP to support cooperation among five countries of North Asia in the Tumen River Area Development Programme (TRADP). One initiative has been a strategic regional approach to sustainable tourism development that includes action programmes to protect biodiversity and the international waters from the impact of economic development. The aim of the Tumen Secretariat's strategic regional approach to sustainable tourism development would be to facilitate measures that minimize environmental degradation caused by tourism and give tour operators the ability to apply the principles of environmental best practices. By cooperating with WTO it would be possible to have a comprehensive human resources development strategy for training and education, a needs analysis and recommendations for a full-scale tourism human resources development project. The project would be designed to use existing resources and give direct benefits to women, youth and disadvantaged groups.

From existing data and estimates, the total amount received from tourism in the Tumen River area countries was about US$ 40.6 million in 1998. Data have not been available for all Tumen River area countries and there has not been systematic study of the economic impact of tourism in the area. Another project of the Tumen Secretariat relates to developing a tourism project for the subregion. One activity involves creating brochures to give an international image to the subregion and attract investment. Meetings on cross-border issues in the transport sector should help facilitate tourist travel by land routes. A working group on transport wa^c scheduled to meet in early September 2000 fc discussions related to land transport facilitation. Som bilateral agreements have been reached about border opening hours. Construction of roads and customs buildings has been subject to pre-feasibility study and some work has already begun.

Recent cooperation in the Tumen River area has focused on understanding the key tourist source markets in order to strengthen the area's potential. One project would train officials from the NTOs in market research. Joint tourism promotions and familiarization tours are being considered. The Tumen River Working Group on Tourism decided to participate with joint representation at the International Tourism Asia Fair in Hong Kong,

China during September 2000. The Tumen Secretariat would support this initiative and WTO would conduct a promotional seminar for the region.

United Nations Development Programme (UNDP)

The UNDP office at Seoul helps facilitate the participation of the Republic of Korea in the Tumen River Area Development Programme (TRADP). As follow up to the Second TRADP Working Group Meeting on Tourism in August 1999, UNDP Seoul organized a meeting to consider various initiatives of the government of the Republic of Korea to support tourism development in the Tumen River area. Support would focus on activities that could help attract tourists from the Republic of Korea. In November 1999, UNDP and WTO supported a familiarization tour organized by the Tumen Secretariat for journalists and tour operators from five countries, including the Republic of Korea. Several strategic barriers hindering the area's tourism potential were identified, particularly impediments to facilitation of travel. In May 2000, participants at the Third TRADP Working Group Meeting on Tourism agreed to develop projects in six programme areas, including joint tourism development planning, international investment promotion, travel facilitation and training and technical exchanges.

United Nations Environment Programme (UNEP)

The United Nations Environment Programme (UNEP) addresses issues and takes supporting action in PASTA's theme area of the environmental management of tourism. UNEP relies on a voluntary approach that includes partnerships, codes of conduct and capacity building. UNEP made a feasibility study in three countries for using the Blue Flag scheme in Asia and the Pacific to set environmental quality standards for beaches and marinas. The study is now under review. UNEP launched a Tour Operators' Initiative in early 2000 to share information, develop training and promote environmental awareness among members. The initiative is now being introduced to Asia and the Pacific. UNEP co-published a manual on cleaner production in hotels and resorts. UNEP and WTO organized a Conference on Sustainable Tourism in the Islands of the Asia-Pacific Region scheduled at Hainan Island, China in early December 2000.

UNESCO's Principal Regional Office for Asia and the Pacific

The United Nations Education, Scientific and Cultural Organization (UNESCO), Principal Regional Office for Asia and the Pacific recently reported on six tourism projects designed to address a combination of the six theme areas of PASTA. One regional project covering pilot sites in nine countries aimed to establish communication between the tourism industry and those who conserve and maintain cultural heritage sites in order to develop sustainable tourism strategies that cover fiscal management, tourism investment, community education and training and resolving conflicts among stakeholders. During all four phases of this project, UNESCO, local governments, educational institutions and PATA would be actively involved. The project clearly involves supporting action on human resources development, economic impact, environmental management, infrastructure and investment and regional cooperation. Local stakeholders prepared in-depth case studies for the pilot sites in nine countries for presentation at a UNESCO regional conference on Culture, Heritage Management and tourism held at Nepal in April 2000.

A second regional project involves UNESCO and PATA collaboration covering seven countries in order to produce a series of site-specific publications that can educate industry personnel, policy makers and site managers about how to develop the tourism industry while preserving the environment and cultural heritage of a location. UNESCO and PATA would produce a series of publications entitled "Impact", which would address issues related to promoting a tourism industry based on responsible community-based management. This regional project covers human resources development, economic impact, environmental management, regional cooperation and other initiatives, including private sector participation.

The Nam Ha ecotourism project involving integrated planning for culturally and ecologically sustainable tourism development through district and local community management is a national project in Lao People's Democratic Republic. In addition to UNESCO support, funds were also available from New Zealand and the World Bank. The project was designed to use tourism as a tool for integrated approaches to rural development that would conserve the natural heritage as well as validate and preserve traditional cultures. Participation and management by the community would help protect the cultural rights of the indigenous people. Another national project of UNESCO involves integrated planning and community involvement for culturally and ecologically sustainable tourism development in and around the Andaman Sea marine and costal protected areas of southern Thailand. The project aims at developing tourism potential in ways that protect the local environment and preserve the ways of life of the indigenous sea gypsies. The first phase of the project has been completed and the second phase would include, among other activities, training of local stakeholders and developing an integrated management plan.

As part of another national project, UNESCO planned to hold a subregional seminar to establish a preservation management plan to integrate protection of outstanding cultural and natural features of the Batanes Archipelago in the Philippines. Site managers from other countries in Asia and the Pacific would share their experiences and expertise to protect marine ecology, encourage active participation by indigenous populations and protect unique landscapes and archeological sites. An integrated management plan would serve as the means to give local communities the knowledge, skills and tools to share responsibility for sustaining the local environment while developing sustainable eco-cultural tourism.

Vigan, Philippines is the location for a national-level UNESCO project to establish a "small business incubator" at a small town near a world heritage site. When Vigan was designated as a World Heritage Site in 1999, increased tourist arrivals created a need for local entrepreneurs to provide tourism-related products and services. UNESCO has been working with the community and the local university to create models on entrepreneurship that would help sustain and preserve a small historic town and provide livelihood opportunities. It is expected that the project would be implemented with help from other partners and private sector sponsorship. The Office of the UNESCO Regional Advisor for Culture implements all projects by working in close coordination with the national commissions for UNESCO in each country.

World Tourism Organization (WTO)

The programmes and activities of the World Tourism Organization (WTO) cover all six theme areas of PASTA and contribute to the sustainable development of tourism at the international, regional and national levels. WTO also has a strong record of effective collaboration and coordination with other international organizations, as well as regional and subregional organizations. The WTO programme in human resources development aims at improving the quality and efficiency of tourism education and training through the TEDQUAL methodology, certification and audits, as well as the General Tourism Aptitude Test (GTAT) certification.

WTO cooperated with ESCAP to organize a Tourism Week at Macao in May 1999, which resulted in the Macao Declaration on Human Resource Development in the Tourism Sector. WTO has also been formulating a long-term Tourism Human Resources Development Plan for the Tumen River Area. One main focus of the WTO has been the development of a tourism satellite account (TSA) to more accurately measure and analyze the economic impact of tourism. A regional seminar on TSA for Asia and the Pacific was held in February 2001 at Bangkok. National seminars and technical assistance on

TSA are also provided to requesting member countries. WTO has also studied the impact of the financial crisis on Asia's tourism sector.

WTO has been working to implement the recommendations from the United Nations Commission on Sustainable Development made in April 1999. This includes cooperation with the Earth Council and WTTC to organize follow-up regional seminars. WTO also organizes national seminars and provides technical assistance on ecotourism and general environmental issues. WTO assists at the national level to support infrastructure development and investment in the tourism sector. WTO recently completed a study on visa facilitation along the Silk Road as part of a project to revive the road as a unique tourism product.

WTO has close collaboration with a large number of international and regional organizations in Asia and the Pacific, whether they are directly or indirectly involved in tourism. Cooperation covers a broad range of activities, including those that support sustainable tourism development. Other related initiatives of the WTO at the regional level have included: International Conference on Cultural Tourism at Siem Reap, Cambodia from 11 to 13 December 2000; cooperation with UNEP to organize a conference in December 2000 held at Hainan Island, China as part of a Programme of Action for the Sustainable Development of Small Island Developing States; publication of Guide for Local Authorities on Developing Sustainable Tourism with a companion volume of case studies from Asia and the Pacific. There is close collaboration between WTO and a number of international and regional organizations, including ADB, ASEAN, ESCAP, IOTO, PATA, SAARC, Tumen

Secretariat, UNDP, UNEP and UNESCO. Cooperative activities cover all six theme areas and can involve joint conferences, seminars, training programmes and workshops.

World Travel and Tourism Council (WTTC)

The World Travel and Tourism Council (WTTC) is a private sector global coalition of chief executive officers from all sectors of the travel and tourism industry. WTTC aims to assist governments in implementing appropriate policies for sustainable tourism development. There have been several initiatives taken by WTTC related to sustainable tourism development at the regional and global level. The major global initiative relates to the Agenda 21 programme for action developed in cooperation with WTO and the Earth Council. One major regional initiative has involved collaboration with the APEC Tourism Working Group to produce and update a report on the economic impact of travel and tourism development in the APEC region. WTTC is also committed to helping implement the APEC Tourism Charter. This includes assistance to develop TSA, independent research to support implementation of the APEC Tourism Charter's action plans, contributing expertise to policy teams who are developing the action plans and setting up a collaborative travel and tourism research consortium for the region or a tourism information network.

WTTC has a Human Resource Center located at Vancouver, Canada to do research about global good practices. WTTC has published simulated TSA for over 160 countries and worked with many Asian and Pacific government in this effort. In 1994, WTTC started the Green Globe environment awareness programme to encourage tourism businesses to make environmental improvements. Green Globe 21 now operates as an independent organization that monitors and certifies businesses. It maintains links to WWTC. There is also a WTTC Infrastructure Task Force working towards the sustainable development of infrastructure. The Task Force is comprised of business leaders and policy makers from around the world. WTTC has a commitment to working for the elimination of bureaucratic barriers to travel and tourism that includes working with other industry associations, immigration authorities and technology suppliers. Together, they have developed and introduced pilot systems for automated screening methods. WTTC policies also focus on trade liberalization and open skies policies.

ESCAP

PASTA provides the overall framework for the work of ESCAP in tourism. The aim is to strengthen national capabilities and promote regional cooperation to bring economic and social benefits to wide segments of society. ESCAP activities at the regional, subregional and national level support implementation in the six theme areas in order to help governments maximize the socio-economic benefits from tourism development while minimizing any adverse impact. The basic forms of ESCAP assistance are studies, workshops and technical advisory missions. ESCAP gives special attention to countries in the early stages of tourism development, including the least developed, land-locked and island countries and areas economies in transition.

ESCAP serves as the secretariat and regional coordinator for the Network of Asia-Pacific Education and Training Institutes in Tourism (APETIT), which was established in 1997 at Tehran, Islamic Republic of Iran. The purpose of APETIT is to promote regional cooperation in human resources development to overcome various problems and constraints commonly faced by developing countries with respect to tourism training and education. The work of APETIT is organized into five activity groups with a member institute acting as the responsible regional focal point for each activity. The five activity groups are:

(1) information management,

(2) communication links,

(3) training and advisory services,

(4) sharing experiences and

(5) research and development.

ESCAP has cooperated with APETIT member institutes to organize two meetings of APETIT's General Council, one at Macao, China in May 1999 and one at Khajuraho, India in August 2001. There have been six meetings of APETIT's Executive Committee. As of August 2001, the membership of APETIT now comprised 120 tourism education and training institutes and organizations in 33 countries. The Second Meeting of the General Council at Khajuraho, India reaffirmed that human resources development in tourism, especially training, played a vital role in the sustainable development of tourism and that efforts should be exerted to make APETIT beneficial to as many members as possible. The Meeting recognized that APETIT member institutes would greatly benefit should the scope of the APETIT work programme be expanded to encompass wider areas of training, such as ecotourism, environmental management system, General Agreement on Trade in Services (GATS), etc. However, the Meeting affirmed that member countries and areas would be responsible for creating and designing education and training programmes according to their respective needs and priorities for tourism sector development.

ESCAP also organized a Seminar on Tourism Education and Training in the Asia-Pacific Region at Khajuraho for APETIT members. The Seminar covered a number of topics, including training needs for sustainable tourism destination management and the involvement of stakeholders in tourism education.

One area of special focus was on countries with tourism industries at an early stage of development, which faced constraints in their tourism education and training systems. Countries in the early stages of tourism development were encouraged to take a number of remedial actions that would enable their education and training systems to respond to the growing demands of their tourism sector. While most of these measures were the responsibility of each country and area, cooperative efforts through APETIT could also be encouraged and developed.

A second area of special focus at the Seminar was the Pacific subregion, where countries displayed great diversity and unique obstacles to the delivery of training across vast geographical distances. An overarching framework for tourism training and education development in the Pacific could help address challenges to human resources development.

The South Pacific Tourism Organization (SPTO) had recently commissioned a Regional Tourism Strategy with a component on human resources development that underlined the need for regional tourism training standards. This would require closer working relationships between regional and national tourism training organizations, as well as public and private sector stakeholders, and APETIT could serve as one vehicle for establishing networks of training and education relationships. APETIT is a successful cooperative endeavour in the Asian and Pacific region in view of the rapidly increasing membership, the growing number of activities involving sharing and exchange and the continued donor support. ESCAP has also published two studies on human resources development. One was on regional cooperation in human resources development in the Asian and Pacific region and one on human resource development requirements of the tourism sector in India.

Reliable research and systematic understanding of the economic impact of tourism is important for improved policy-making and integrated planning. From 1990 to 1996, ESCAP prepared a number of country studies and a regional overview in order to gain more systematic understanding of the economic impact of tourism based on input-output analysis. The regional overview highlighted three main patterns to the economic contribution of tourism in ten Asian countries. Countries with the first pattern showed a strong economic impact on income, but a low economic contribution. The second pattern showed a relatively weak impact on income, but tourism made some contribution to the economy. The third pattern was a moderate impact on income, but a mixed economic contribution. A number of countries have yet to study this issue area and need to build their national capacity to do such research. This would enhance the opportunities to share information and experiences as well as compare policies and actions.

ESCAP has organized regional meetings and national seminars in order to strengthen national capabilities in environmental management and the promotion of ecotourism. These activities have been in response to a greater awareness among Asian and Pacific countries and areas that tourism places special challenges on the ecology. Moreover, it is recognized that the environment is a tourism resource affected by other economic activities. Systematic, well-coordinated management aimed at sustaining the environment and preserving tourist destinations requires planning, legislative, institutional and other measures. Awareness of this point has guided the work of ESCAP within the framework of PASTA.

ESCAP has organized several national seminars on sustainable tourism development. The National Workshop on Sustainable Tourism Development in China, held from 1 to 2 November 2000 in Tianjin, China, aimed at promoting better understanding of the issues related to sustainable tourism development, including ecotourism. Presentations and discussions at the Workshop focused on identifying ways and means to balance sustainable tourism development with environmental protection and how to make proper use of local resources, targeting the western provinces of China in particular. The Workshop was organized in collaboration with the China National Tourism Administration with financial assistance from the Government of Japan.

Community-Based Tourism Development and Coastal Tourism Management in Indonesia was held from 27 to 28 June 2001 in Jakarta, Indonesia. The purpose was to enhance national capabilities to take action in order that tourism would be economically viable, socio-culturally acceptable and environmentally sustainable. Actions should result in movement towards responsible tourism that would bring benefits to wide segments of society. Particular emphasis was on actions that focused on community-based tourism in coastal areas with marine environments as a way to broaden social participation and good practices based on public-private sector partnerships. The Seminar was organized by ESCAP in cooperation with the World Tourism Organization (WTO) and the Indian Ocean Tourism Organisation (IOTO) in collaboration with the Department of Culture and Tourism of the Government of Indonesia.

The National Seminar on Sustainable Tourism Development in Myanmar held from 30 to 31 August 2000 in Yangon, Myanmar, was held in order to enhance national capabilities for taking effective measures to promote tourism with an emphasis on sustainable tourism development. Presentations and discussions covered issues related to integrated tourism development and the challenges faced by Myanmar in sustaining tourism development. The potential of the private sector and how to strengthen its role in making tourism development sustainable was also considered. The Seminar was organized jointly by ESCAP and WTO, in collaboration with the Ministry of Hotels and Tourism. The Government of Japan provided financial assistance.

ESCAP has been cooperating with the WTO and PATA to help strengthen national capabilities to develop tourism infrastructure through investment, public-private sector partnerships and policies that encourage investment. One regional seminar held at Bangkok in March 2000 through joint efforts of ESCAP, WTO and TAT focused on public-private partnership in tourism development. A Regional Seminar on Expanding the Economic Benefits of Tourism through Promotion of Investment in Tourism Infrastructure was held at Seoul, Republic of Korea, in May 2000. WTO and PATA contributed to the Seminar by providing resource persons. Infrastructure development for the tourism sector is a relatively new area of ESCAP's work. However, ESCAP has been doing studies and organizing national seminars on investment, the role of the private sector and the potential for public-private sector partnerships for sustainable tourism development.

ESCAP can provide support at the regional level for countries and areas that seek to make full use of tourism's development potential by overcoming travel impediments and procedural constraints. Such constraints might relate to visa policies, frontier formalities, customs regulations, and safety and security measures. ESCAP has made country-level studies on facilitation of travel and conducted regional seminars. ESCAP, WTO, IOTO and PATA have been collaborating to assist in removing barriers to tourism and facilitate travel. Activities at the subregional level have included a Seminar on Expansion of Tourism in the Greater Mekong Subregion through Improved Air Transport in July 1999 at Vientiane. ESCAP co-sponsored an Asia-Pacific Conference on Tourism for People with Disability held in Bali, Indonesia in September 2000. One important outcome of the Conference was the Bali Declaration on Barrier-Free

Tourism for People with Disabilities in the Asian and Pacific Region. Promotion of barrier-free tourism in the region should focus on related legislation, education and training to raise awareness and sensitivity, and provision of accessible facilities in the tourism sector.

APETIT is one of the most useful and successful mechanisms for regional cooperation in Asia and the Pacific. From 1997 to 2001, as noted above, its membership has increased from 23 to 120 training and education institutes in 33 countries and areas. ESCAP has supported a number of bilateral and multilateral cooperative activities involving APETIT members through TCDC. Since 1995, ESCAP and ADB have jointly supported the Working Group on the Greater Mekong Subregion Tourism Sector, comprised of NTOs from six countries along the Mekong/Lancang River. The Working Group has been meeting annually, the Agency for Coordinating Mekong Tourism Activities (AMTA) was set up within TAT in Thailand and a wide variety of other activities have been undertaken based on cooperation with UNESCO, PATA, AMTA and ADB. ESCAP has taken the lead role in organizing national and regional seminars on tourism marketing and promotion, facilitation of subregional travel, sustainable tourism development and ecotourism in the Greater Mekong subregion.

2

Assessment of Asia-Pacific Tourism

The Asia-Pacific region has been one of the most dynamic for international tourism over the last decade and the potential for further growth over the medium and long term remains strong. It currently accounts for around one-eighth of all international tourist arrivals but a somewhat larger share - approaching one-fifth - of international tourist receipts. Following the financial crisis of 1997, when tourism to the region temporarily collapsed, international tourism had been steadily regaining lost ground until the security incidents of September 2001.

While China was the clear front-runner, almost all countries saw growth in international tourism volumes and/or receipts. Since then, the region has, in common with most other regions of the world, borne the brunt of economic slowdown in the world's main generating markets as well as a widespread unwillingness to travel far from home as a result of concerns over safety and security, including income and job security. However, the region as a whole topped the growth rankings for 2002 -

up by almost 8% - but in reality only some countries - notably China, Thailand and Islamic Republic of Iran, as well as Hong Kong, China, and Macau, China - managed to maintain strong growth trends.

The impact of recent uncertainty caused by the Iraq war and the SARS outbreak makes it difficult to predict when the region will regain its former dynamism. The region's main tourism destinations, judged in terms of international tourism receipts, are China, Australia, Thailand, Republic of Korea and Singapore. Between them these five countries account for around half of the region's total receipts - some US$44.4 bn in 2001 (out of a regional total of US$87.2 bn) - and received almost 39 million arrivals (out of a regional total of 90 million). This is not to deny the relative size and importance of the industry in many of the smaller destinations, of course, with the industry playing an increasing role in countries such as Cambodia and Viet Nam and in small island states in the Pacific region.

The World Travel and Tourism Council (WTTC) is currently the only source of interrelated estimates of tourism GDP, export revenues from tourism and employment in tourism. WTTC distinguishes between the "travel and tourism industry" and the "travel and tourism economy". In effect, the former deals with the direct effects of tourism only and the latter with the direct plus indirect impact. This is especially important in estimating employment. Employment in the "travel and tourism industry" includes all activities in direct contact with visitors such as airlines, hotels, car rental activities, restaurants, retail and entertainment activities.

WTTC's definition of "travel and tourism economy" comprises, in addition:

— suppliers to the industry (e.g. airline caterers, laundry services, food suppliers, wholesalers, accounting firms and so on which have some involvement with the tourism sector);

— government agencies, manufacturing and construction of capital goods and exported goods used in the travel and tourism sector; and

— supplied commodities (e.g. steel products, lumber, oil products and so on which are used in the travel and tourism sector).

The contribution to the travel and tourism economy of these sectors is included on a proportionate basis as derived from input-output matrices for the economies concerned.

The Hotel Survey, carried out in April/May 2003 among a selection of the major international hotel groups which have operations in a number of different countries in the Asia Pacific region. The selected groups tend to operate relatively large hotels at the mid- to up-market levels and therefore, by individual establishment, employ large numbers in comparison with many other businesses within the sector. While not purporting to be an accurate representation of the experiences of all hotel operators, the survey results provide a reflection of some of the views or concerns of the largest global hotel companies operating in the region. The respondents were given an assurance of anonymity in order that their views could be expressed more freely. Responses were obtained from five hotel groups, which together account for over 200 hotels and 70,000 hotel rooms in the region. In addition to the responses received from the head office human resources managers, the human resources manager at individual hotels also responded to the survey in many cases.

While Macau, China, and the small island nation of Fiji rely particularly heavily on the tourism sector, tourism has an above-average importance in a number of countries, notably New Zealand, Thailand, Australia and Cambodia. When the indirect effects of tourism are included, the sector's importance to GDP typically rises to between two and three times the level of the direct contribution shown below, although there are some considerable variations in this relationship country-by-country.

As the tourism market in the Asia-Pacific region matures, it also accounts for an increasing share of world outbound travel - representing around 17% of all international arrivals in 2001. Travel intensity remains low, however, at 3 trips per 100 population (compared with a world average of 11 trips per 100). The region generated almost 121 million international arrivals in 2001, three-quarters of which (77%) were to destinations within the region itself. Japan is head and shoulders above any other outbound market in terms of both volume and expenditure (accounting for a little less than half the whole region's expenditure), but this market has been in the doldrums over the last few years. Proving particularly strong over the last two years have been China, Hong Kong, China, India, Republic of Korea and Viet Nam. Data on Asia-Pacific intra-regional expenditure are not readily available. However, daily expenditure per capita on outbound tourism by travellers from the region is estimated by the World Tourism Organization to be US$26 (compared with a world average of US$75), a spending figure that is likely to be much smaller for travel within the region itself.

Emerging Trends in Labour Market

World Travel and Tourism Council estimates have covered employment levels in each major Asian and Pacific country on an annual basis since 1998, both for direct jobs in the sector (the "travel and tourism industry") and for direct plus indirect jobs (the "travel and tourism economy"). In 2003, 38.7 million people worked directly in the industry across the region, and that an additional 76.1 million were indirectly employed, giving a total of 114.8 million dependent on the sector or more than half of the estimated 195,000 jobs in the world's depending on the travel and tourism sector directly or indirectly. China and India by their very scale dominate these figures. Together these two countries have 78.2 million employed in total in the sector, of which 25.1 million are direct employees of the industry and the balance, 53.1 million, indirectly employed. Thus all the other countries of Asia and the Pacific, excluding India and China, have 36.6 million jobs in travel and tourism, of which 13.6 million are direct and 23.0 million indirect.

Direct travel and tourism employment has declined since 1998, by over 5%. The decline in China and India (in particular the latter) has been less marked than in many other countries in the region, while Singapore has seen the largest decline, and Indonesia, Pakistan, Philippines, Viet Nam, Thailand and Nepal have seen falls of over 10% in the period. On the other hand, increases in direct travel and tourism employment were registered in almost half of the countries, of which those in Brunei and Malaysia were by far the most important. These trends may be due to more than one influence. The 1997 financial crisis in Asia left behind it a legacy of economic slowdown which hit employment levels hard. There may also have been improvements in labour productivity through an application of labour-saving technologies and work organization within this period.

There is some evidence to suggest that the tourism industry might be contracting more work out to suppliers, thereby diminishing direct employment but raising indirect employment, since the trends in total "travel and tourism economy" employment are different from those in the "travel and tourism industry". There has been an increase of 3.8% in total direct plus indirect travel and tourism employment since 1998, dominated by gains in China and India (742,000 new jobs). In China, although the country has been booming as an international tourism destination, the overwhelming influence has been domestic travel. According to the China National Tourism Administration, there were 810 million domestic trips (leisure trips only) in 2002, double the number recorded in 1993; Chinese tourism is reported to be growing faster than the Chinese economy as a whole, and tourism is clearly a major source of labour demand as a consequence. With the exception of China and India, however, total labour demand in the travel and tourism economy fell by 2.6% between 1998 and 2003, representing an absolute loss of almost 1 million jobs.

In 2003, direct employment in the region's travel and tourism industry accounts for 2.3% of all employment, while direct plus indirect jobs accounts for 6.9%. By global standards, these figures remain a little below average. Worldwide in 2003, WTTC estimates that direct employment accounts for 2.8% of all jobs, and direct plus indirect for 7.8%. The labour market in Macau, China, depends to the greatest extent on tourism, with direct employment in the industry representing 26.6% of all jobs, and direct plus indirect 68.4%. This is exceptional, given the special status of Macau, China, as a centre for leisure and gaming. Elsewhere in the region, the highest proportion of direct employment, is in New Zealand, Australia, Japan and Thailand. Taking indirect and direct jobs together, however, the top four are New Zealand, Australia, Islamic Republic of Iran and Japan.

Finding and retaining staff is a key area of concern for employers in the tourism industry. A number of trends emerging in the labour market are common to many countries throughout the region. These can be summarised under the headings listed below.

— *Industry image*: Generally throughout the region, as with most other places in the world, the image of the tourism sector, and particularly hospitality, is rather low and it is not regarded as an attractive industry in which to work. Other sectors such as the financial sector or IT prove far more appealing, particularly to the younger generation. Employment in hotels and restaurants is regarded as offering low pay, unsocial hours, shift work, work over holiday periods and sometimes the necessity to work away from home in remote resorts. For those with some training in the sector, working abroad or on a cruise ship may offer an attractive alternative. It appears that as the number of educated youth grows, they prefer to avoid the service industries. In particular, the lack of a career path acts as a deterrent. However, in a few countries such as China, there was some feeling that employment by the large international hotel companies carried a certain kudos and provided an international exposure that was appealing.

— *Gender*: Generally the employment of females in the hospitality sector is higher than in many other industries, in part reflecting the high percentage of low skilled jobs in hotels and restaurants such as waitresses, chambermaids and so on. As a broad generalisation, the ratio between male and female employees in the Asia-Pacific region is fairly equally split. Among the Hotel Survey respondents, there was no indication that female recruitment was more difficult than male. In China mention was made of legal regulations protecting female workers.

— *Mobility of labour*: For the majority of the emerging economies, there is - in terms of numbers - an ample supply of local labour for all sectors of the tourism industry. Asia's financial crisis of 1997 and the ensuing economic downturn has also meant that unemployment has risen in places such as Hong Kong, China, that previously had labour shortages. Malaysia, for example, which previously welcomed foreign labour, has now introduced severe restrictions, sent some workers home and made some jobs off-limits for foreign workers. This labour surplus means that there is a ready supply of workers for all low skills jobs although there are clearly shortages of suitably qualified personnel at the mid-range and higher skills levels. For more skilled openings, particularly at managerial and professional level, most companies noted that there was a need to import labour from abroad. Hotel companies in China, Malaysia and Indonesia made specific mention of the lack of qualified personnel at this level. They noted that the procedure for importing labour could be time-consuming and sometimes difficult. However, in all cases, it was felt that the transfer of technology and knowledge skills was an important element in their staff development.

Countries vary in the controls they place on the importation of labour, but invariably place different caps for certain types of grades. Generally, in the more developed economies, the less skilled the opening, the more difficult it is for the foreign worker to gain an entry permit. In many cases employers need to demonstrate that it is impossible to fill a post with a suitably qualified local before the employment of a foreign worker is allowed.

— *Skills shortages:* Low worker commitment and a shortage of skills are the most frequently cited problems facing the industry by both the trade itself and by industry practitioners and organizers. Many employees lack interest in their job, have no business direction and demonstrate little initiative. Turnover rates tend to be high. In most countries there are skills shortages across the board ranging, at the lower skills level, from fast-food cooks to waiters and waitresses to bar attendants to chefs. In Hong Kong, China, for example, training in Chinese catering is one of six sectors specifically selected by the government for those with secondary education or below. Particular mention was made of the need to train chefs in specific cuisines in order to cater to the tastes of the increasingly cosmopolitan traveller. Skills at management level were particularly lacking in many countries and a shortage of those with leadership qualities appears to be a common problem in most destinations.

— *Language training*: An inadequate proficiency of foreign languages among staff and potential workers needing face-to-face contact with guests was a recurrent theme for most destinations. This was the case in most countries, and became more acute for employees working away from the capital and major gateway cities where they had less exposure to foreign languages and less opportunity for language training. First mention was made in almost all destinations of the need for workers to be able to operate in English, reflecting the universal language of tourism. However, depending on the major markets for a destination, Asian languages are becoming increasingly important. Languages mentioned included Mandarin, Japanese, and even Russian.

— *The policy environment*: In the Hotel Survey, most respondents in most countries described the policy environment within which the hotel sector operates as "supportive". Nonetheless it was also common for comments to be made along the lines that governments could do more to help identify skills shortages, improve the supply of trained staff, and that governments could have a role, together with the industry, in seeking to make the hotel sector a more attractive place in which to work.

— *Enterprise size:* The tourism sector is characterised by a high percentage of small and medium sized businesses. Indeed in many less developed countries, there are also a considerable number of operations such as food vendors and trinket sellers that do not fall within the formal economy at all. A particularly common feature of the tourism industry is a high number of working proprietors.

Generally it is only the more up-market hotels and the tourist offices in the larger destinations that

> employ relatively large numbers. The majority of one-, two- and three-star hotels, restaurants, and other ancillary businesses such as car hire operations, travel agents and retail outlets are generally small businesses with low numbers of employees. Singapore exemplifies the picture in a more developed destination - which has a significant number of four- and fivestar hotels - where, despite this, over 58% of hotels and 84% of restaurants employ fewer than 25 persons. In Sri Lanka, registered hotels and restaurants employ an average of only 36 people, while tour operators and travel agents employ an average of 12, and recreational agencies and tourist shops have on average just four and five employees respectively.

Data on employment in Asia-Pacific countries are given below. They are generally not comparable between countries, due to different definitions and statistical concepts, as well as the different methodology of the primary sources.

Australia: According to the Australian Bureau of Statistics' Labour Force Survey, there were some 9.5 million people employed in Australia in June 2003, representing a participation rate of slightly under 64%. In addition, just over 600,000 people were unemployed, which implied an unemployment rate of 5.9%. Of the 12 million people in the age range of 15-69, 40% (4.8 million) have post-secondary school qualifications. Of these, 27% hold degree-level or higher qualifications, 22% have an undergraduate or associate diploma qualification, 35% hold a skilled vocational qualification and 16% a basic vocational qualification. By and large, the Australian labour force is stable in most industries, with staff turnover not generally regarded as a problem.

Australia's Tourism Satellite Account provides considerable detail about the make-up of employment within the tourism sector. In the consultation paper for the 10-year plan which has been instituted by the Minister for Small Business & Tourism, it is pointed out that around 70% of employees in the travel agency and accommodation sectors are female, against a national average of 44%, and that part-time workers in cafes and restaurants account for 70% of all employees compared with a national average of 26%.

The tourism industry in Australia has a strong component made up of small and mediumsized businesses, as is the case in other countries. In Australia, over 88% of businesses in the accommodation, cafés and restaurant sector, and over 95% of businesses in the cultural and recreational services sector are classified as small businesses employing fewer than 20 people. In addition, there are a large number of non-employing owner-occupier businesses within the accommodation, cafés and restaurant sector.B

Bangladesh: The results from the Hotel Survey indicate that there are few recruitment problems within the country, although a shortage of management skills does arise. No importation of labour is necessary for most jobs within the hotel sector, and there is reported to be no particular difficulty in recruiting female staff for appropriate positions. However, it is expected that labour market issues will become increasingly difficult to solve in future, and the comment is made that employment growth may be inhibited by wages tending to be rising in the industry.

China: China's labour market is estimated at well over 700 million people at the end of 2002. It is estimated by the Ministry of Labour and Social Security that the level of unemployment is 7%, caused in part by the restructuring of state-owned enterprises. The government estimates that an economic growth rate of 7% a year will be necessary merely to absorb the excess labour shed from these enterprises. In 2000, 42.9 million Chinese were employed in the "wholesale, retail and catering" sector - a further breakdown is not available. However, in the state sector only, there were 1,158,000 employed in hotels, of which 671,000 (58%) were female, in "tourism" the total was 122,000 of which 57,000 (47%) were female, and in recreational services, the total was 66,000 of which 36,000 (55%) were female. Although these are small numbers only in the context of the total labour force, the proportions indicate that female job opportunities in the tourism sector are considerable.

For the hotel and tourism industry, a key issue is that of providing staff able to operate in a foreign language - most usually English. This is reported to be relatively straightforward in the major urban areas such as Beijing and Shanghai, where college graduates are relatively plentiful and English language capabilities exist, but it is far harder to find such staff elsewhere in the country. In general, it is in China's fastest growing regions, such as the south and the emerging cities of Tianjin, Hangzhou, Chengdu and Shouzhou that a shortage of educated and skilled labour is most marked.

A respondent to the Hotel Survey - a major global company with extensive interests in China - states that there are difficulties in recruiting food and beverage staff within China, especially at the executive chef and food and beverage management level. However, what are described as "rank and file" staff can be found because "the hotel business attracts staff generally and provides international exposure and career development opportunities" which are welcomed within the country.

A respondent from another international hotel company claims that staff recruitment in China can be a problem, especially with regard to foreign language capabilities (notably in English) for those jobs which involve face-to-face contact with guests. A third respondent broadly makes the same points, but adds that financial staff with English language abilities are in short supply, as are waiters and waitresses. Important enterprises in China used to be either state owned enterprises (SOE) or foreigninvested enterprises (FIE) forming two different labour market segments. Nominally, employees in a state owned enterprise have to seek permission to leave their jobs, making transfers from one sector to the other difficult. However, in practice this procedure is less rigidly enforced than in the past, and it is now easier to transfer.

As in addition, fringe benefits such as automatic provision of free, life-time housing which used to characterise jobs in the SOE's begin to break down, it is felt that these two labour market segments will eventually merge into one, improving labour mobility within China, Also, as Chinese workers become better educated and more proficient in language skills, FIEs are increasingly inclined to hire Chinese nationals rather than automatically to think of importing expatriates.

Hong Kong, China: Towards the end of 2002, the labour force in Hong Kong, China, estimated by the Census and Statistics Department to be some 3.5 million was suffering an unemployment rate of over 7%. Approximately 43% of the labour force is female, 57% male. While the workforce is generally well-educated, there is concern about a growing shortage of highly-qualified, mainly university level, people; projections indicate a shortfall of this grade of up to 120,000 people by 2006, in response to which various educational initiatives are being taken as well as a programme to attract more, highly qualified individuals from the Chinese mainland. A characteristic of the employment pattern in Hong Kong, China in recent years has been an erosion of the manufacturing base, as many manufacturing jobs have moved to mainland China. At the end of 2001, for example, there were nine service sector jobs for every one manufacturing job, a trend that is expected to continue.

In mid-2001, the government of Hong Kong, China, initiated the Skills Upgrading Scheme, allocating HK$400 mn to a programme aimed at raising competences for workers with secondary education or below. Among the six sectors identified as priorities is Chinese catering. Training courses in all of these began in September 2001 and in November the scheme was extended to include tourism and hotels, as well as property management and hairdressing.

Immigration for work purposes is generally easier for managerial, professional and entrepreneurial skills than for less skilled occupations. Nonetheless, the Supplementary Labour Scheme allows for the immigration of workers who fall outside the general policy on entry for employment. Companies may be able to import workers provided they can show that they have given priority to locals and that they are genuinely unable to recruit from the local market. They must also have advertised the posts locally, undertaken four weeks of potential job matching with the Hong Kong, China Labour Department and sought staff via the tailormade retraining courses for workers who are available. By the end of 2001, under this scheme 8,750 people had been admitted to Hong Kong, China, since the scheme's inauguration in February 1996. A respondent in the Hotel Survey indicated that the overall standard of English language ability gives some cause for concern, and also that the company had found a shortage of experienced cooks for their hotels' operations.

India: According to the Department of Tourism, Government of India, there were some 12 million people employed directly in the tourism sector at the beginning of this decade. The point was made that tourism has a very positive capital to labour ratio, with 89 jobs being created in the hotel and restaurant industry per 1 million rupees of investment, compared with 45 jobs in agriculture and 13 jobs in manufacturing. By 2010, the Government of India has identified that as many as 6 million additional jobs in the tourism sector may be created, most of which will be generated by domestic tourism demand (which, very much along the same lines as in China, far outweighs the importance of international tourism; in 2001 some 190 million domestic trips were made in comparison to international tourist arrivals of 2.5 million). Thus the need for tourism training and education could become a key issue in the expansion of the sector.

Indonesia: Hotel Survey results for Indonesia indicate, in common with a number of other countries, that finding suitable staff for the hotel sector is difficult. There is a view that school education provides inadequate "business orientation" for the industry, whereby it is claimed that employees in the sector often do not seem to be equipped to take the initiative but require constant and close direction. On the positive side, recruiting female staff appears not to present a major problem. One respondent stated that there is a shortage of staff in the following skills areas: - food and beverage management, culinary staff), and engineering staff. Another respondent to the Hotel Survey provided an extensive list of employment policy issues which indicates, in this respondent's opinion, that the Indonesian labour market suffers from some strong disincentives to the recruitment of permanent (established) staff. The respondent claims that there is too much job protection which makes shedding labour in the current difficult circumstances very hard, and thus encourages fixed term contract recruitment rather than the conclusion of permanent contracts. Among the concerns cited are "regulations regarding termination pay, even when employees have been dismissed for unacceptable conduct such as theft; the fact that pay is related to length of service rather than productivity, that an established job is regarded as permanent to the incumbent until retirement; and that severance pay rules are so high that employers cannot afford to reduce the size of their labour force even in hard times."

Japan: The labour market in Japan is changing in the face of a decline in manufacturing activity, economic stagnation and industrial restructuring. Although traditions are hard to shake, the expectation that a new recruit would have a job with the same employer for life has been changing for some time now. There is a greater degree of flexibility in the labour force, partly reflecting jobs that are increasingly subject to globalization tendencies or characterized by technological developments, and partly reflecting economic weaknesses. Although foreign companies report some difficulty finding experienced engineers and middle managers, there is no indication of any shortage of labour within the tourism industry.

In broad terms, Japan encourages the recruitment of labour from abroad where foreigners possess technological skills and knowledge, while unskilled foreign workers are generally unwelcome. The effects of this approach are seen in an analysis of the 670,000 foreign workers who were in Japan in 1999. 252,000 were classified as "overstayers"; workers of Japanese descent, most numerously from South America, accounted for a further 221,000, part-time students for 47,000 and "others" for 25,000. The balance of approximately 125,000 comprised "professors, artists, religious activity, journalists, investors/manages, legal/accountancy, medical, researchers, instructors, engineers, specialists in humanities, inter-corporate transferees and skilled labour".

Macau, China: Total employment in "hotels, restaurants and similar establishments" according to Macau, China, government data rose from 21,700 in 1999 to 22,900 in 2001, having declined slightly in the intervening year. These levels exclude many of the other sectors of activity, such as transport, which are included in the preceding WTTC data. Macau, China, government data for 2002 show the distribution of employment in the travel and tourism sector by gender. Government statistics indicate that, in the accommodation sector, small businesses are reserved mainly for the lower grade hotels and for guesthouse types of accommodation. Higher-grade hotels follow international practice by having relatively large units - the higher the grade, the greater the number of employees per unit.

However, commentators believe that, in the longer term, Malaysia will continue to suffer from skill shortages which may have to be met from abroad. Respondents to the Hotel Survey provided extensive information about employment and labour market conditions across the country's hotel sector. It should be pointed out that some of the issues raised may reflect local rather than national conditions. No hotel reported any difficulty in recruiting staff in general, but there is also a clear indication of skills shortages within the sector. Mention was made of:

— room staff (e.g. chambermaids, stewards);

— food and beverage staff (notably, waiters and waitresses);

— cooks (mention was made of Chinese cooks and bakery staff); and

— housekeeping and laundry operations staff.

Generally, skills shortages within the Malaysian hotel sector are ascribed to factors such as: the unpopularity of hotel work due to long and unsocial hours compared to, for example, factory work; high staff turnover due to many new hotels opening and inducing employees to "job hop" and a lack of suitably trained and competitive candidates, which is blamed by employers on inadequate standards within government education and training services. There was some indication that the recruitment of female staff was not easy, although the majority of respondents did not regard this as a problem.

The majority of responding hotels did find it necessary to import labour, noting that the number of foreign workers is limited by the government. Several also reported that procedures to obtain imported labour could be difficult and time-consuming. Permission needs to be obtained from local government representatives and it is said to be often easier to obtain such permission for "resorts" as opposed to hotels, and that permission is often only granted for clearly specialised skills that may not be available locally.

New Zealand: According to Statistics New Zealand's Household Labour Force Survey, migration contributed to an increase of the working population in New Zealand by around 2% in 2002. The unemployment rate, which has been steadily declining in recent years, fell to 4.9%. The labour force is highly mobile and there is no statutory retirement age. Tourism is reported by New Zealand's Ministry of Tourism to support more than one job in ten in the economy. There are currently an estimated 94,000 full-time equivalent (FTE) jobs and 69,000 indirect jobs in the sector. The industry is reported to be made up of ten major publicly listed companies and close to 18,000 SME's.

The government's Tourism Satellite Account for 1997-99 provides a breakdown of employment within the industry. In the year ending March 1999 there were 86,000 full-time equivalent jobs (FTEs) in the tourism industry, representing 5.6% of the country's total employees. Around a third of jobs are in the accommodation, café and restaurants sub-sectors. Among the FTEs, over 17,000 are attributed to working proprietors (19%), reflecting the substantial bias of small businesses that make up the tourism sector.

Philippines: According to the Republic of the Philippines' National Statistics Office, the Philippines labour force was estimated to amount to around 33.6 million in October 2002; around 30.3 million were classified as employed. Some 37% are employed in agriculture, 15% in industry and the remainder in the service sector. Unemployment in the country is high and increasing - 10.2% in 2002, compared with 9.6% two years earlier. The National Statistics Office predicts that an additional 850,000 will join the labour force annually to 2010. The Philippines economy has traditionally benefited from remittances from the substantial number of nationals working overseas; this sector, however, is facing increasing competition from other labour supplying countries. The workforce has a high literacy rate and - particularly pertinent for the tourism sector - good English language proficiency. The supply of professional, technical and skilled workers is generally adequate.

The National Statistics Office notes that employment in hotels and restaurants in the Philippines amounted to 2.4% of the country's workforce at the end of 2002. At around 712,000, this was a slight increase on the figure of a year earlier. Respondents to the Hotel Survey noted that they experienced no difficulty at all in recruiting suitably qualified staff in the Philippines. There is an abundance of local labour on which to draw, both at the skilled and unskilled levels, and as a result they found no necessity to import labour from other countries.

Generally, the regulatory environment is regarded as very supportive with a Labour Code in force which is considered rather favourable to workers. The hotels reported that it is equally easy to employ both male and female labour. The hotels did, however, express some concerns over labour issues becoming a greater problem in the future. Mention was made of the likelihood of issues such as wages and labour rights becoming challenges for outsourcing labour as the sector expands.

The Philippines Department of Labour is currently working on stringent measures regarding this issue, which may affect hotels' inclination to contract outsourced services.

Singapore: Singapore's workforce is reputedly one of the most stable and productive in Asia. Adverse economic conditions in 2001 led to a slowdown in employment growth which has continued 2002. Unemployment increased to 4.4% by the end of 2001, according to Ministry of Manpower, and remained broadly at that level throughout 2002. Older and less-educated workers have been the worst hit by rising unemployment. Nonetheless, Singapore's workforce is ageing rapidly and there are fewer economically active people in the younger age brackets. To address this, the retirement age was raised to 62 in 1999, with the intention of raising it to 67 in due course. According to the government's Labour Force Survey, there were a total of 125,325 persons employed in the hotels and restaurants sector in Singapore in 2002, representing 6.2% of the country's total workforce. Figures for 2000 show that over half (56%) of those were in direct service occupations, such as waiters/waitresses, bellboys, front office staff etc., and a further quarter were in housekeeping and cleaning occupations in hotels. As a result of manpower shortages, however, there is a high degree of multi-tasking in the restaurant sector, in particular. Some 14% of workers in the sector are employed on a part-time basis.

The hospitality sector, as elsewhere, attracts a relatively high proportion of female labour. There is an almost even ratio of females (48.5% in 2000) to males (51.5% in 2000) working the hotels and restaurants sector which compares with a 39:61 ratio for the workforce as a whole. It is noticeable that there is a higher proportion of younger (15-19 year olds) and older 50 years and over) workers - particularly women - in the hotels and restaurants sector compared with all sectors generally.

The occupation breakdown for hotels and restaurants is as follows:

— service and sales workers 56%

— cleaners and related workers 25%

— clerical workers 7%

— professionals and managers 9%

— technicians and associated occupations 3%

Average earnings in Hotels and Restaurants are the lowest of any category in the formal sector. In 1999 the average monthly earnings for workers in the economy were S$2,813, while in Hotels and Restaurants they were only S$1,291. They have also been the most sluggish in terms of growth: average wages increased by 56% for all sectors in the economy, while for hotels and restaurants the growth was half that. In 1999 there were some 3,400 establishments serving the tourists. In the hotels sector, there a fairly wide range of sizes of enterprise, while the restaurant sector is dominated by small establishments. One-third of all hotels employed more than 100 people but two-thirds of restaurants employed fewer than ten.

Hotel companies in the Hotels Survey reported that they experienced difficulties in recruiting suitably qualified staff, and the ability to attract those with leadership qualities and sufficient skills and experience - especially of the hotel sector - is a big problem. For most management positions, suitably qualified managers are available locally. However, the service sector is not popular among Singaporeans and shift work is especially unpopular. This is particularly the case among the younger generation who prefer other more glamorous industries such as IT and banking. Recruitment for the private sector is not made easier by the fact that government employees are offered high salaries and incentives. Hotels also report high staff turnover rates. Because of the mis-match between jobs and staff availability in Singapore, hotel companies find it necessary to import labour from abroad. However, there is a government-imposed quota for non-skilled workers and restrictions by sector or industry. Hotels are also faced by a set higher-salary requirement for skilled or professional workers. There is a belief in the industry that this situation is unlikely to improve and as a result, labour issues will become increasingly difficult. An added problem, they note, is the fact that the gap between young workers and old workers is not closing up because of Singapore's small workforce.

Small island states: Most of the small island states of the South Pacific are more than normally dependent on the tourism sector - particularly since the discontinuing of trade preferences on commodities such as sugar and fish, for example - and tourism is one of the few sectors that offers development potential. Across the region generally, the growth in populations, and of younger age groups in particular, together with a decline in semi-subsistence living, has led to an increase in the numbers seeking paid employment which has not been matched by an availability of jobs. Tourism is one of the biggest sources of employment, not only in major destinations such as Fiji and Tahiti but also in smaller countries like Kiribati, Niue and Tuvalu. The South Pacific Tourism Organization (SPTO) suggests that tourism provides up to 15-20% of employment in several South Pacific countries. The industry is characterised by a predominance of SME's but the overall number of tourism enterprises is relatively small, estimated at around 1,500 in total. In the accommodation sector, if the small number of large hotels is excluded, the average number of rooms per establishment is just 15.

The South Pacific Tourism Organization, in its 2001-05 Business Plan, states that the bulk of the SME's are run by family operations. It also draws attention to the fact that in the context of the South Pacific, tourism offers opportunities to both male and female entrepreneurs, especially in the case of ecotourism, to establish businesses within their natural and cultural framework. In some cases, the report notes, "the wife and children are the main players, running small family operations. In most cases, rental cars, travel offices and booking agencies are dominated by female entrepreneurs."

Sri Lanka: In early 2002 Sri Lanka's labour force consisted of 7.3 million workers (Department of Census and Statistics, Department of Labour), of whom some 8.7% were unemployed. Two thirds of the labour force is male but unemployment among females is double that of males (12.8% compared with 6.5%). The labour force is literate and educated, but lacking in certain technical skills. Unemployment is much higher among the better educated; for those educated to GCE (A/L) and above, the rate is 16.7%, while for those below Grade 5 it is only 2.1%. Most permanent workers are covered by laws relating to minimum wages, hours of work, the right of association and health and safety standards.

A Termination of Employment Act makes is almost impossible to fire workers who have been employed for more than six months, other than for cases involving serious disciplinary problems. Child labour is prohibited and is virtually non-existent in the organized sector. Some 35% of labour in the industry and service sector is unionized. There were nearly 38,000 people directly employed in 1,312 different establishments in the tourism sector in Sri Lanka in 2000. As a result of the poor performance of the tourism industry in 2001 following the bombing at Bandaranaike airport, direct employment reduced to 35,400. Indirect employment was also down - 49,600 compared with 53,100 in 2000. Official figures indicate that every direct job in the tourism sector generates 1.4 indirect jobs.

hTe number of employees in tourism establishments increased over the two-year period by over 7,500 workers although there was a reduction in the number of businesses in 2000 compared with 1998 by some 26 (primarily tourist shops). Nevertheless, small and medium-scale enterprises predominate, with the average number of workers per business at 29; if the airline industry is excluded, this is reduced to 26. By sector, the average number of employees per hotel is 36, while for travel agencies and tour operators it is only 12. The majority of employees working in the tourism industry - some 67% of the total - are employed in the hotels and restaurants sector. Around 11% work in tour operators and travel agencies, and a further 12% work for airlines. Over half of all employees work in technical, clerical and supervisory jobs, although within the hotel sector, one-third of workers are unskilled.

Thailand: According to Thailand's Labour Force Survey, there was a total labour force of around 34.6 million at the end of 2002. Unemployment is low, at just 1.8%, having dropped sharply, from 4.8% at the beginning of 2001. The two main problems facing the government are a shortage of skilled labour - further aggravated by the fact that recession has forced many children to leave school prematurely - and rising labour costs to levels well above those of trading rivals like China, Malaysia and Viet Nam. Employment in hotels and restaurants accounted for around 6.1% of the country's total workforce at the end of 2002.

A survey conducted by the Tourism Authority of Thailand (TAT) in 1997, shows employment in the following five groups:

— unskilled and semi-skilled (37% of the total);

— basic skilled level (28%);

— technical (supervisory level) (25%);

— mid-management level (5%); and

— management level (6%).

The majority of those working in the industry were at the younger end of the age scale (21-30 years) and there was a relatively even split between male and female. Most had graduated from primary school, high school and vocational school. Despite the very low rate of unemployment in Thailand, the Hotel Survey respondents reported little difficulty in recruiting suitably qualified staff for most types of posts. Several hotels did, however, mention that there was a shortage of suitably qualified nationals who offered leadership skills to take up managerial roles. It was also noted that recruiting employees for guest contact positions who had good English language skills could be a challenge.

Due to the generally good supply of local labour, almost none of the companies had experienced a need to import labour from abroad, although it was mentioned that some positions requiring certain skills or language proficiency did necessitate this. One hotel group noted that it was sometimes not easy to obtain permits for workers from South Asia or the Middle East. For the future, it was envisaged that the recruitment of qualified staff would become more difficult, particularly as many of the good staff were attracted by working overseas in Thai restaurants or as cabin attendants on cruise ships.

Viet Nam: The labour force is growing rapidly, at around 2.5% a year, and unemployment is a problem. Around 60% of the population is of working age, with government forecasts indicating that this will rise to 70% by 2010. Half the population is aged 15-34. Although there is a large pool of workers which is generally literate and hard-working, there is a skills shortage; according to MoLISA (Ministry of Labour Invalids and Social Affairs), only 16% of the workforce were classified as "skilled" in 2000, i.e. had some form of training or tertiary education, and only 4% had university qualifications. The service sector accounts for around 20% of employment.

Governments' Role in Tourism Development

For most of the countries in Asia and the Pacific, tourism is acknowledged to be an important part of the national economy and is accorded some priority within governments. Obviously, this importance varies. In small island states, tourism may be the dominant economic sector; at the other end of the scale, such as in more industrialised countries, tourism generally has a lower political profile. In all countries, however, one of the key features of tourism is its capacity to create employment.

To generalise again, foreigners spend some A$1.3 bn annually in Australia and thus generate worthwhile economic benefits in addition to performing a useful function for the tourism industry.

China: Tourism in China is regarded as being of national importance and is subject to detailed planning, mainly under the aegis of the China National Tourism Administration (CNTA). It is fair to say that, while tourism from abroad is important to China in terms of its contribution to foreign exchange earnings, it is domestic tourism which dominates the country. The country has a 20-year tourism development plan, and has declared its intention to transform itself from an important regional tourism destination within Asia into the world's largest tourism destination within the next 20 years. The government states that it sees tourism as an important component in the national economy, and it is seeking to develop the sector accordingly. Policy documents have been issued on the subject and, in 1999, it was decided to designate three "gold tourism weeks" - based around National Day, May Day and the Spring Festival.

While much of China's tourism business is nationally owned, in acknowledgement of the country's entry into the World Trade Organisation, China has started to admit foreign-owned travel agencies. These numbered eight in 2000. For outbound travel, China designates individual countries as approved destinations for its citizens travelling for leisure purposes; this list included 21 countries by 2002 and is likely to expand further. The CNTA has a role in identifying training and human resource needs and promoting the training and educational support required to meet these.

Macau, China: The Macau Government Tourism Office (MGTO) is funded directly by the government under the Secretary for Social Affairs and Culture. The MGTO has a wide range of responsibilities, including the formulation and implementation of tourism policy, improving the quality of service through tourism industry training programmes, and the protection and enhancement of the value of local tourism resources. MGTO also encourages and promotes activities beneficial to tourism, promotes inbound Macau tours in relevant origin markets, and has the responsibility for building relationships with international organisations. It suggests legislation related to tourism to the government and monitors the activities of operators to ensure their compliance with the relevant tourism laws; it also licenses tourist venues and activities. The MGTO in addition has licensing and inspection powers for accommodation, ranging across all the hotel grades and three of the five grades of non-hotel accommodation (such as pensions), the remaining two grades coming under the control of another organ of the state.

New Zealand: In New Zealand the Ministry of Tourism was established in January 2002 from a previous agency, the Office of Tourism and Sport. It is a semi-autonomous body within the Ministry of Economic Development, with direct policy reporting to the Minister of Tourism. The prime aim of the Ministry is to maximise the benefits to New Zealand from the sustainable development of the industry; this latter aspect is regarded as especially important in New Zealand and hence its "100% Pure New Zealand" marketing stance. The main role of the Ministry is to provide tourism policy advice to the Minister of Tourism. It works with other government departments on policy issues and provides tourism research and statistics for the benefit of the industry and the broader investment community. It also provides advice on government investments, administers grants and assists with major events. A key role is to continue to raise awareness of the importance of tourism's contribution to the economy.

The Ministry itself has little statutory or regulatory responsibility, and as a result relies on developing relationships and educating a wide range of other government departments on their impacts on tourism. The Ministry has an annual budget of NZ$5.38 million for 2003/04 and a staff of 15 advisors and researchers to fulfil these functions. Marketing activity undertaken by the government is carried out through Tourism New Zealand (TNZ). TNZ's international marketing activity includes tourism brand building, advertising and promotion, the international media programme, trade training, participation in trade shows, running an internet site and provision of market research.

The direction for New Zealand's tourism was set out in The New Zealand Tourism Strategy 2010 launched in May 2001, hailed as a "landmark document". It contains a comprehensive set of principles and objectives covering all facets of the industry. The aim is stated to be the maximisation of the industry's tourism potential "while ensuring cultural, social, environmental and economic sustainability". If the funding recommendations of the plan are carried out, it is projected that tourism earnings (domestic and international) could increase from NZ$8.9 bn in 2000 to NZ$26.8 bn in 2010; (without implementation of the new strategy, the Tourism Strategy Group predicts that earnings would only reach NZ$15.7 bn).

Training in the Tourism Sector

While there is wide agreement on the need to improve the supply of well-educated and -trained staff for the travel and tourism industry, it is also clear that resources are lacking. Often, there is an absolute shortage of trainers, and the attraction of top quality trainers is often hampered by low public-sector pay scales within the training and education sectors. In terms of best practice in the identification of skills needs and in the organisation of industry training schemes, Australia, China and Singapore are undertaking country-wide programmes, with Australia in particular leading the way in the design, planning and delivery of training programmes across the industry and especially at the vocational, non-academic levels.

Generally, it is at this level that skills shortages are most apparent. Since many jobs in the industry do not require academic qualifications, and also because there is generally a shortage of government and private sector vocational training schemes, in many countries the major hotel groups and travel companies tend to rely on their own in-house training abilities. This does not help the many small businesses in the industry, however, who cannot afford the luxury of in-house trainers. The provision of suitable training programmes for SMEs is therefore a matter requiring specific attention.

Some of the generally applicable issues that have emerged from many of the countries covered below include:

— *Quality of training*: There is concern over the quality of many of the training courses on offer; this partly reflects, in some countries, the lack of national standards (or at least of their enforcement), partly the shortage of well-qualified trainers for the reasons outline above and partly an absolute shortage of resources to fund training centres and programmes.

— *Relationships with the industry:* In a number of countries there is concern about the lack of contact between the travel and tourism industry and the academic establishment which is responsible for higher level training and education, indicating a need for central authorities such as the relevant government ministries or the national tourist office, depending upon the distribution of responsibilities, to take the lead in improving cross-sectoral co-operation.

— *Career development concerns*: Even where lower-level training is broadly satisfactory, there is concern over a lack of skills upgrading and opportunities for life-long learning. The point is made that it is often difficult for staff to progress through the organisation that employs them. For example, hotel staff working in rooms or food and beverage operations can find it hard to advance themselves to more senior levels. If this situation could be improved, it would create a "virtuous circle", by providing better opportunities for skills upgrading. This could help to eliminate the perception of an industry which offers poor career perspectives, thereby improving its ability to attract new recruits.

Some key data on staff-training in the Asia-Pacific countries are given below:

Australia: At the end of the 1990s there were estimated to be 3,800 students engaged in tourism and hospitality studies at a variety of Registered Training Organisations

(Australian schools of tourism and hospitality). These included many from outside the country whose own countries did not offer such skills training themselves. Tourism industry training in Australia is in the hands of Tourism Training Australia (TTA) - described as a "joint industry, government and union national training body". TTA has a major role in the definition of skills needs and shortages within the Australian tourism industry. TTA has produced a 20 year forecast of skills development needs, and has identified national skills shortages in skills such as:

— pastrycooks (28,400 people are employed as bakers and pastrycooks where earnings are low - in the third decile);

— bar attendants (54,600 employed with earnings in the second decile);

— chefs (48,900 employed, with earnings in the fourth decile);

— cooks and fast food cooks (employing respectively 39,000 and 22,000 people with the lowest earnings of all - in the first decile); and

— food and beverage attendants (waiters and waitresses, where 98,800 are employed and earnings again are in the lowest decile).

TTA rates vacancy levels as "average" for pastrycooks, "high" for chefs and "very high" for the remainder of these skills. The current and future training programmes for the industry reflect these priorities. Overall, TTA estimates that 16,000-17,000 new cooks are required by the industry every year, against a current recruitment rate of 13,000-14,000 a year. There is also a shortage of language skills in some of the jobs which have face-to-face contact with tourists, notably for Asian languages such as Japanese and Mandarin in areas such as tour guides and hotel staff. TTA estimates that an additional 1,200 tour guides are required annually.

Australia, under the aegis of TTA, has developed a range of National Training packages which were introduced in 1996 and which address a wide range of course requirements across all aspects of the tourism industry. As part of its long term development plans, TTA has developed a wide range of courses across the country targeted at the skills shortages and anticipated future needs which its detailed forward planning has identified. Other institutions and bodies, such as the Australian Hotels Association, Restaurant and Catering Australia and the Australian Federation of Travel Agents also conduct training programmes.

Bangladesh: In Bangladesh a respondent to the Hotel Survey stated that there is no government hotel school as such, although the National Tourism Training Centre has been used by the company to recruit some staff, nor is there any "credible" private sector source of hotel industry training. As a consequence, the company concerned undertakes most of its training on an inhouse basis.

China: In China, there is a national programme for tourism training. According to the China National Tourism Administration (CNTA), at the end of 2000 there were 1,195 tourism colleges and schools with a total of 328,000 students. Of the 1,195 colleges and schools, 252 offered tourism vocational courses which had attracted almost 74,000 students; 96 of these colleges offered courses in tourism management. In that same year, 782,000 employees in the tourism industry participated in various training programmes, including on-the-job training for administrative personnel, professional training for technical workers, adaptation, overseas and adult schooling training. Of these 782,000, some 555,000 came from tourist hotels, 168,000 from travel agencies and 20,000 from tourist bus and shipping companies.

China has a National Association for Tourism Colleges and Universities and a National Association for Secondary Tourism Vocational Schools. These organisations co-operate on the development of curricula. CNTA also provides trainers within China, and has sent trainers to many parts of the country to help in regional and local training initiatives. National qualifications are offered at a variety of levels. In 2000, over 9,100 people took part in qualification authentication for travel agency work, of whom 6,500 received qualifying certificates. There were also examinations for:

— general manager qualification certificates for international travel services (with over 950 passes);

— department manager certificates in the same area (over 1,360 passes);

— general manager and department manager courses for domestic travel services (over 2,400 and 1,780 certificates respectively);

— over 100,000 people succeeded in the national guide qualification certificate for tourist guides; and

— CNTA's system for hotel vocational English language training attracted 4,500 students and a pass rate of just over 50%.

Respondents to the Hotel Survey, among others, identify difficulties in recruiting staff offering reasonable competence in the English language. A recent example of a new approach is the joint venture that has been established under the name of "Tourism Training Institute at Tsinghua Science Park", between the Tsinghua University, located in the city of Zhuhai adjacent to Macau, China, and the Tourism Training Institute of Canada. The latter is a division of Global Education in Tourism Ltd., a company based in Vancouver on Canada's west coast. Courses will be offered from the second half of 2003, which are part of the American Hotel & Lodging Association's Educational Institute Programme and will offer opportunities for work experience overseas.

Macau, China : Tourism industry training in Macau, China is led by the publicly owned Institute for Tourism Studies (IFT). This was established in 1995 and had the distinction of being the first educational institution to be granted the Themis TedQual (Tourism Education Quality) attestation by the World Tourism Organization. It is the only higher educational establishment operated by the Macau government specifically for the tourism and hospitality industries. The IFT is also the authorised training centre in Macau for the International Air Transport Association (IATA) which certifies IATA-standard staff in travel agencies. The Institute for Tourism Studies delivers its services though two institutions - the Tourism College of Macau (TCM) and the Professional and Continuing Education School (PACES). The TCM provides higher diploma and bachelor courses in hotel and tourism business management, while PACES focuses on entry and supervisory level training in five areas - Travel, Hospitality and Catering, Management, Customer Service Development, and Languages and Communication.

The authorities in Macau, China expect demand for employment in the travel and tourism sector to grow rapidly, by between 7,000 and 10,000 jobs in the next two years - due to the liberalisation of the gaming industry and to the opening of new hotels. In order to provide the labour required for this expansion, the Institute for Tourism Studies has combined forces with the Polytechnic Institute of Macau to establish the Macau Tourism and Casino Career Centre. This body will commence operations in the second semester of 2003, and has as its objective the provision of additional training opportunities to those wishing to join the industry.

Part of the Macau, China government's approach to tourism development is the imposition of quality standards. For example, tour guides are requested to attend a 180 hour training programme run by the IFT, all travel agencies in Macau are required to have a technical director with related qualifications or 3 years' relevant experience, and all taxi drivers must pass a special examination set by the Macau Civil and Municipal Institute in order to obtain their licenses.

Malaysia: The training experience and practice from five hotels within one company in Malaysia, as revealed in the Hotel Survey, shows that the same company can adopt a variety of approaches according to local needs and standards. Two out of five undertook only in-house training, only one used government schemes, and four out of five used the private sector. It is noticeable in these responses that Malaysia offers a wide range of training institutes and organisations for the hotel sector, including schemes operated by the Ministry of Tourism, public bodies such as the Human Resources Development Council and associations such as the Association of Hotel

Employers, together with a wide range of private training organisations and companies. These latter address both general and specific skills, such as information technology, and include national companies as well as foreign companies which have branches within the country.

New Zealand: There are reported to be in excess of 750 providers of tourism training courses, including secondary schools, in New Zealand. There are also three industry training organisations serving the tourism sector - Sports, Fitness, Recreation Industry Training Organisation (SFRITO), Aviation Tourism and Travel Training Organisation (ATTTO) and Hospitality and Service Industry Training Organisation (HIS). In the view of the Tourism Strategy Group, set out in New Zealand Tourism Strategy, 2010, rationalisation is required. The large number of training organisations results in fragmented training provision and makes it difficult to communicate the needs of the sector to training providers. The current delivery of training, it notes, does not suit either SMEs or their employees. In addition, the training content does not focus sufficiently on planning, establishing and managing businesses effectively and it is not provided in a way that makes it accessible to SMEs.

The Strategy Group also draws attention to the fact that the nature of much tourism-related employment can exacerbate capability issues for the sector. Tourism generally is not regarded as an attractive long-term prospect for employment and the loss of experienced staff and low recognition of tourism's value to local communities and to the country has a negative impact on sector capability. The Group recommends that better learning opportunities and more portability of skills within the sector should be provided. The image of the industry also needs to be raised and awareness increased of its role and importance. Other recommendations include the establishment of a process to enable the identification of sector-wide skill requirements and effective workforce planning, the need to make the development of SME and Maori tourism participants' capability a top priority, and the need to co-ordinate training opportunities and build capability at a regional level. The Strategy paper also notes that Skill New Zealand's funding for tourism training is disproportionately low when compared to the sector's contribution to the economy. In 2000 Skill New Zealand allocated only 1.1% of total funding for industry training to aviation, tourism, travel and hospitality. This compared to 10.1% to agricultural training and 9.1% to forestry.

Philippines: The premier training establishment in the Philippines is the Asian Institute of Tourism (AIT), part of the University of the Philippines, which offers four-year degree courses in tourism. There are, in addition, around 120 other schools offering degree courses, as well as numerous others offering degrees in Hotel and Restaurant Administration and Management. There are also many vocational and technical schools and other institutions providing training, which is supplemented by in-house training programmes offered by hotels, resorts, restaurants and tour and travel agents in specific sectoral skills.

In general the manpower supply for the industry in terms of quantity is adequate. More of a problem is the quality of courses provided. In 1999 it was noted by the University of the Philippines, Asian Institute of Tourism, that out of the 120 schools offering a four-year degree course nationwide, only 31 were accredited by the Commission on Higher Education, the office which grants state recognition to schools of higher education. Part of the problem lies in the training provided. There is a severe shortage of qualified teaching staff and generally a lack of resources for tourism training and facilities. In addition, there is a need to forge links between the industry and academia in order to match the training of students with the requirements of the industry.

A number of other training programmes require mention:

— *The Technical Education and Skills Development Authority (TESDA), a* government agency involved in human skills development, has linked up with the Department of Tourism and the private sector to develop skills training, curriculum development, accreditation, standardisation and certification. The TESDA also provides scholarships for skills training.

— *The Department of Tourism offers* a range of tourism programmes, including housekeeping, food handling, tour guiding, tourism awareness, foreign languages and marketing and communications.

— *The Tourism Industry Board Foundation is* a tripartite body composed of representatives of government, the private sector and labour set up to promote human resource development. The TESDA has subsidised most of the training programmes and the development of occupational skills standards (OSS) and trade tests undertaken by the Board.

Another government/private sector institution is the Hotel and Tourism Institute of the Philippines, an initiative involving the Hotel and Restaurant Association of the Philippines and the Department of Tourism.

TESDA in co-operation with a number of selected tourism training institutions and the German Agency for Technical Co-operation has introduced a project to promote Dual Training at all levels in technical schools and training centres throughout the country.

The Department of Tourism, supported by American Express, operates the Mabuhay Super Host Program, which aims to teach front office staff skills. Respondents among the different companies in the Hotel Survey - which, it should be stressed, were international hotels operating large establishments - indicated that almost all training took place in-house and virtually no use was made of either public or private sector training establishments. The exception to this was the necessity of sending employees such as engineers and plumbers for training in order to update their licences, as required by the law. Both government training and private/ commercial training establishments were used for this purpose.

Singapore: The Singapore government is attempting to upgrade its post-secondary education facilities, with greater emphasis on technical, vocational and commercial education. The aim is to have about 40% following technical and vocational courses at polytechnics, 20% undertaking academic courses at university and 25% studying at the Institute of Education. Currently there is a high proportion of workers in the hotel and restaurant sector with below average educational qualifications, reflecting the fact that nine out of 10 occupations in the sector are service, clerical or cleaning related activities. For such positions, in-house training of a suitable candidate is regarded as more appropriate than academic qualifications. However, there is an increasing emphasis on the need for workers to upgrade their skills to bring about a higher standard of service quality.

Singapore's Ministry of Manpower and the economic agencies conducted a national survey in 1999 to gather feedback from employers in the hospitality sector on the employment situation, including the amount of training being provided and the skills they would require in their workers in the next two years. The most frequently cited requirements were:

— Degree - Degree in Business Studies/Administration (with Hospitality Customer Service Modules)

— Diploma - Diploma in Tourism

— Diploma in Business Administration

— Specialised Skills - Knowledge in Food and Beverage Operations

— Knowledge in Hotel Management

— Generic Skills - Customer Service Skills

— Supervisory Skills

— Human Resource Management Skills

— Sales Management Skills

The hotels sector tends to require higher educational qualifications than the restaurant sector for managerial, professional or technical positions. Generally a university degree is required in hotels, while a diploma is sufficient for a similar position in a restaurant. For administrative positions in hotels, a diploma in hotel or hospitality management is often required, while for executive positions secondary education is sufficient, although some hotels prefer diploma holders. In the restaurants industry such positions generally require only secondary education. For clerical and service jobs in both sectors, secondary education is the norm.

Training opportunities in the sector include the following:

— *SHATEC courses*: the Singapore Hotel and Tourism Education Centre conducts short part- ime programmes from one to eight days, customised hospitality programmes, and full time courses offering diplomas in tourism studies and hotel management.

— *Skills Redevelopment Programme (SRP):* The Singapore Hotel Association (SHA) and National Trades Union Congress are jointly responsible for training courses designed to upgrade the skills of workers in the hotels industry in areas such as housekeeping, food preparation, F&B service etc. Courses vary in length from a few weeks to a few months.

— *National Skills Recognition System (NSRS)*: this programme was launched by the Singapore Tourist Board (STB) and the Singapore Productivity and Standards Board in 2000 to strengthen and enhance job competencies. Under this scheme, workplace skills standards for the hotel industry have been developed and training to meet these standards accorded recognition. About 130 competency standards for the hospitality sector have been identified. Up to the end of 2001, 788 hotel employees had been certified in 13 Units of Competence.

Temasek Polytechnic and the STB are working on e-learning programmes in lodging and catering A range of other educational establishments (such as Ngee Ann Polytechnic) and training centres (such as Comat Training). In order to attract more to join the sector and alleviate the manpower shortage problem (a problem that was more acute up to 2001), the STB and SHA have undertaken programmes to create awareness of career opportunities in the sector. Hotel companies approached in the Hotel Survey noted that, in addition to in-house training, they used both government training establishments and commercial training centres to train their staff.

Small island states: In terms of human resource development, the islands of the South Pacific suffer from their small size and their isolation. A lack of local management expertise and poor service quality are frequently expressed criticisms of the regional industry. A Tourism Council of the South Pacific (TCSP) review undertaken in 1995 identified the following three key issues:

— low levels of training activity across the region, with an over-reliance on government parastatal provision; investment in people was not receiving the priority it deserved;

— limited public awareness of the current and potential benefits of tourism;

— the training provided was not always relevant to requirements.

Tourism training facilities in the region are limited. Seven countries have no institute for formal training. Generally the quality of the training and the facilities are also not of a standard comparable to more sophisticated tourism destinations. In addition, among those countries that do have training establishments, there is no region-wide certification and standards vary widely. There is a particular need for training aimed at small enterprises such as guesthouses and tour operators, and for community-based tourism in rural areas. A 1999 TCSP review identified the need for school-based training for clerical, management and cookery skills, and particularly noted waiting, cooking, housekeeping and bar tending. However, it is often difficult to persuade employees to move away from their villages to attend training courses, so on-the-job training becomes of greater relevance. Hotel managers, however, are unwilling to invest in training when margins are low, which can lead to a vicious downward spiral.

Human resource development is a major part of the activities of the TCSP. It has trained 14,000 travel agents in seminars and workshops, and 7,000 people in hotel and catering services, marketing, tourism awareness and management. As at mid-2001, it had three trainers, specialising in food production, food service, housekeeping and front office, as well as offering courses for tour guides. The University of the South Pacific based in Fiji and covering 12 countries in the region, also offers a basic Certificate in Tourism Studies as well as degree courses.

Sri Lanka: Sri Lanka has one public sector training institute, the Ceylon Hotel School & School of Tourism, managed by the National Tourist Office, which offers training for the hospitality and tourism sector at all levels. It has an annual output of around 1,200 students. The central school is located in Colombo, and a number of satellite schools have been opened in the provinces with the aim of training some of the educated but unemployed youth in the regions. There are also several private sector training institutions. However, the provision of training facilities is regarded as insufficient for the industry's requirements and considerable training is undertaken in-house by the major hotel chains. No comprehensive courses are available for the training of tour operators and travel agents. A particular problem is the fact that training institutions find it difficult to attract quality staff. The government sector is the largest training provider in Sri Lanka and government salary scales are such that high calibre staff is not attracted. At the same time, the industry does not have an attractive image and as a result other industries prove more appealing for quality employees.

Thailand: In a speech delivered at a conference on Human Resource Development in the Asia-Pacific organised by the World Tourism Organization in 1999, Mr. Suwat Jutakorn, the Director of Hotel and Tourism Training Institute of the Tourism Authority of Thailand (TAT), noted that the industry badly needed to upgrade the quality and numbers of both skilled and unskilled workers in the hospitality and tourism sector if it was to meet international standards. This was particularly the case at the operations level. One major problem, he noted, was a lack of proficiency in foreign languages to deal with foreign guests, particularly English, Chinese, Japanese and Russian. This general lack of training was also mentioned by hotels responding to the Hotel Survey who noted that even among staff who had ostensibly received training and had hotel vocational or technical certificates, there was usually a need to train them (again) from scratch.

TAT itself had introduced a programme to promote education in the industry and was undertaking research into a number of issues related to human resource development, such as curriculum development and the demands of the labour market. It had also set up a network of education and training institutes in tourism in Thailand to be responsible for research, information and development. However, the industry is challenged by a shortage of experienced instructors and the fact that many teachers are of poor quality, study materials are in short supply, curricula need standardising and modifying and by the fact that educational establishments fail to co-ordinate either with each other or with the industry they represent.

In order to address some of the problems, TAT established the Hotel and Tourism Training Institute (HTTI) with the assistance of the International Labour Organization (ILO) and the United Nations Development Programme (UNDP). The HTTI has co-operated with various educational institutions both in Thailand and abroad, such as Australia, Canada and Switzerland, in order to improve and develop the quality of education standards through teacher and student exchanges and professional contact. It offers a large number of courses across many sectors of the industry and ranging from two year courses offering Higher Certificate of Hotel and Tourism to short courses from one year to a few days.

Respondents to the Hotel Survey in Thailand reported that, in addition to in-house training, they use a wide range of both public and private sector training establishments. Within the public sector mention was made of courses offered at State Universities, the Ministry of Industry, Ministry of Energy, the Thai Red Cross Society, the Metropolitan Electricity Authority and the Engineering Institute of Thailand under His Majesty the King's Patronage. Within the private sector, training took place in a wide variety of disciplines such as human resource management, computer skills, engineering, live saving and so on. One hotel group noted that it imported outside instructors or suppliers to train its staff.

Security Management

Any major disruption to the security or safety of any tourist destination - from natural or man-made threats - will have an immediate effect on demand for visits to that destination and a sharp impact through the loss of employment in tourism and related industries, not least because some jobs in the tourism industry are seasonal, temporary or casual, and thus staff can easily be shed when markets weaken. If the situation lasts longer, not only employment gets lost irretrievably but enterprises are threatened in their existence. Especially small and medium-sized enterprises are threatened to disappear as they cannot rely on sufficient capital to survive longer periods of reduced demand for their services. The effects on employment and the well-being of enterprises in tourism destinations can be attenuated if the tourism authorities succeed in managing the situation well. The constituents of the International Labour Organizations, at the Informal Meeting held in October 2001 emphatically recommended tripartite cooperation to mitigate the social impact of slumps in tourism demand. Experiences made in different countries recently are too fresh to be assessed comprehensively.

Bali: The Asia-Pacific region has had its share of man-made disasters that have had an adverse impact on tourism. Most recently, the security incident of 12

October 2002 in Bali overnight turned one of the region's most successful destinations, and one which was especially popular with Japanese and Australian tourists, into a place from which most tourists had fled. Prior to the incident and despite economic weaknesses and a loss of confidence in international travel occasioned by the events in the United States on 11 September 2001, tourism in Bali was booming.

In the four month period May-August inclusive, during which approximately 43% of annual international arrivals come to the island, there were 538,000 arrivals in 2000, 551,000 in 2001 and 592,000 in 2002, an increase of 10% in two years. Tourism is the mainstay of the Balinese economy and its success created large numbers of tourism-dependent employment on the island as well as elsewhere in Indonesia. Arrivals in Bali in the early years of the current decade were around 1.4 million a year, some 27% of all international arrivals in Indonesia.

In employment terms, Bali had around 50,000 hotel workers and 18,500 restaurant workers prior to the security incident, in addition to 33,000 people working in the wholesale trades and 314,000 in the retail trades. The proportion of the Balinese employed labour force working in these four sectors was 24.2%; in Indonesia as a whole, these sectors accounted for 18.2% of all jobs, indicating how important tourism is for the island's economy. Informal estimates suggest that 40% of the island's jobs depend on the tourism sector; others that 80% of households depend on tourism. Few data are available on the aftermath of the security incident in October 2002 specifically in terms of employment, but it is clear that demand for tourism to the island remains very depressed. As an indication of its effect on demand, however, in January 2003 there were only 60,000 arrivals compared with 110,000 in the same month of the previous year.

In the immediate aftermath of the Bali incident, hotels found occupancy levels falling to negligible levels. Employees were required to take all unused leave, to take "leave in advance" and to reduce their working days, all of which were seen as "preludes to the seemingly inevitable staff reductions" which would arise if the crisis of confidence were to continue, according to the Executive Chairman of Indonesia's Culture and Tourism Board. The Minister of Manpower announced that "up to 130,000 hotel and tourism workers were likely to be laid off" within a month of the attack. It was also made clear that the impact of the incident would not be confined to Bali. Other regions of the country with strong migration, labour market or supply linkages to Bali in regions such as Central and East Java, and Lombok, would also be affected. It was expected that international tourists would also stay away from attractions in other parts of the country, such as Yogyakarta and Lombok.

The Minister of Finance estimated that at least 10 sub-sectors - including hotels, land and maritime transport, restaurants, entertainment, tours and sightseeing, souvenirs, health and beauty services, and tourist guides - would suffer. The World Bank Country Officer for Indonesia stated that, as a direct consequence of the incident, "...by the end of 2003 there could be 2-3 million more Indonesians living below the poverty line than would have been the case without the attack".

The small beginnings of a recovery in the first quarter of 2003 have now been damaged further by the SARS outbreak in Asia, the continuing uncertainty over peace in the Middle East and by a new warning from abroad (in mid-April 2003) of a further terrorist threat on the island. Before those new threats arose, the Balinese and Indonesian tourist authorities had undertaken a variety of tasks intended to assist the country's recovery as a tourism destination.

At the same time, the region had rallied to do what it could to assist in the tragedy in its midst. Immediately following the bombing, the Pacific Asia Tourism Association (PATA) sent in a senior member of staff to lend practical assistance to managing the situation. An emergency task force of regional experts encompassing a variety of tourism sectors was assembled by PATA to assist the Indonesians. The PATA Bali Recovery Task Force was charged with giving practical advice on how Bali could accelerate the healing process and move the tourism sector onto a path of recovery. Based on the experience of past events and the team's individual areas of expertise, a list of recommendationswas assembled on how the recovery could be stimulated over the short and medium term.

In the immediate aftermath of the bomb, the government provided a safety net through block grants to ensure that Balinese residents received subsidised rice, and additional school and healthcare programmes. In terms of dealing with the tourism crisis itself, the authorities quickly announced a range of actions which followed international experience from previous tourism disasters. Included in these were four steps, described as comprising the four stages of rescue, rehabilitate, normalise and expand. Under the rescue heading was included a rapid switch of marketing emphasis to domestic tourism markets and regional markets within the ASEAN group of countries.

Experience has shown that a key requirement in these circumstances is to keep up a flow of accurate, factual information to tourism markets and tourism companies. This information should present a consistent picture from a single source - confusion and contradiction add to the difficulties. The message distributed should also, wherever possible, provide a positive indication of how the problem is being tackled and what steps are being taken by the authorities to rectify matters. The Indonesia Culture and Tourism Board (ICTB) immediately (the day after the bomb) set up a Media Centre in Bali and Jakarta to act as the communication and information centre for the press, tourism industry and the public. The ICTB also held meetings with seven of Europe's largest tour operators to keep them informed and discuss possible solutions to the crisis.

Plans for the rehabilitation phase included marketing initiatives, fiscal incentives, a media campaign, familiarisation trips for journalists and travel trade representatives, a programme to raise standards across the board, making use of the time available during the drop in activity, reductions in the costs of electricity in Bali's tourism sector, in the cost of the airport departure tax, in parking and handling fees for airlines at the airport and various other tax and fiscal incentives aimed at stimulating the market.

Sri Lanka: Sri Lanka's tourism industry has, more than many, been troubled by crisis incidents over the years. An internal military and para-military conflict plagued Sri Lanka over two decades. As a result, the country's tourism industry is no stranger to initiating crisis management measures in order to deal with the fallout on the industry at home and to handle the negative publicity that has been generated overseas.

However, an attack at Bandaranaike International Airport in July 2001 was especially severe and appeared to hit at the very heart of tourism itself. The airport is effectively the only entry point to the country for international tourists. The incident killed some 17 people and caused the airport to shut down for over 24 hours.

International flights from Sydney, London, Berlin, Rome and the Middle East were diverted. The government had to appeal for calm and asked people in Colombo to remain in their homes. Such measures hit the international headlines and tourism collapsed. Prior to the airport attack, Sri Lanka's tourism industry had been growing, reaching an alltime high in 1999. Numbers climbed from 302,000 in 1996, to 366,000 in 1997, 381,000 in 1998, 436,000 in 1999 and then dipped to 400,000 in 2000. The announcement of peace initiatives in the island encouraged the industry in early 2001 to adopt a new strategy to facilitate effective image and product repositioning, adopting an integrated approach with all stakeholders.

By June 2001, the first six months of the year had seen an increase of 17% on the same period in the previous year, with 227,205 arrivals. However, following the attack, the country's major leisure tourism markets in Europe, notably the UK and Germany, as well as Australia and the USA, saw huge reductions. Total arrivals fell by 14.1% in July, 54% in August, 62% in September and 52% in October; it was eleven months after the incident before growth resumed. The number of tourists travelling by SriLankan Airlines declined by 41% during the second half of 2001, recording a decline of 9% for the year as a whole. Charter flights to the country bringing in leisure tourists declined sharply, accounting for 3% of total traffic in 2001 compared with 7% the previous year.

The sequence of measures undertaken following 24 July 2001 fell into three phases: crisis management activity, damage control measures, and recovery strategies. Immediate action was undertaken to persuade foreign countries to withdraw travel warnings and lower the insurance risk premium imposed on foreign airlines and shipping companies. At the same time, an assessment was made to evaluate the impact in all areas including loss of income, employment and tourism revenue, and how to assist existing businesses through the crisis. The government introduced a relief package to cover temporary difficulties faced by companies through the rescheduling of loans and interest payments and difficulties were assessed on a case by case basis.

A press campaign was launched and familiarisation trips to the country were arranged. The lull in tourism activity was reportedly utilised to try to improve the tourism product and service standards. Four months after the crisis, a marketing campaign was undertaken entitled "Buy one, get one free" for FIT (Free Independent Traveller) customers over the November/December period. The number of nights spent by foreign guests in tourist hotels decreased by 23 per cent in 2001. The industry responded to the difficulties by offering low rates and promotional packages and there was a considerable increase in the number of local guests, particularly in the Colombo city and hill country. This increase in domestic travel helped the hotel sector survive the crisis period.

Provisional figures show that employment in tourism declined significantly as a result of the events. It was estimated that in the case of both direct and indirect employment there was a fall of 6.6%, implying that some 2,500 direct jobs and 3,500 indirect jobs were lost. A substantial amount of casual labour in the industry also reportedly lost jobs. The cease-fire and initiation of peace talks have helped to boost Sri Lanka's international image. Coupled with aggressive marketing by tour operators and Sri Lanka Airlines as well as the hosting of international sporting events, this has helped to restore the country's reputation. There has, in addition, been a significant increase in visits from expatriates - many of Tamil origin - taking advantage of the prevailing peace to visit the island. 2002 arrivals were up by almost 17% on 2001, with particularly strong increases coming from within the region. The vital European and US markets had, however, still to regain growth.

Impacts of Severe Acute Respiratory Syndrome (SARS)

The outbreak of the Severe Acute Respiratory Syndrome (SARS), initially in China, in March 2003 provides an example of a need for crisis management in tourism. It also provides a stark reminder of the vulnerability of the travel industry to 'natural' crises, in addition to man-made security issues and the vagaries of the economic cycle. Although SARS was a headline story in the world's press for a relatively short time, in reality it has dealt (and continues to deal) a severe blow to the tourism industry throughout the Asia/Pacific region, the effects of which may be felt for the remainder of 2003 at least.

In ILO's paper established in May 2003, New Threats to Employment in the Travel and Tourism Industry -

2003,it was estimated that SARS together with other factors such as the continuous economic slump worldwide and travellers' security concerns in view of on going conflicts could result in a further 5 million job losses worldwide in the travel and tourism sector in 2003 which, on top of the 6.5 million already lost during the 2001-02 crisis, would take global jobs losses to 14% of direct employment in the industry since 2001. SARS was especially threatening since its epidemiological characteristics were not yet fully understood by science. It thus had the potential of threatening travellers with danger, including the danger of the unknown, whether or not it had the potential to become a widespread epidemic in public health terms. The nature of the threat from SARS was therefore one of personal safety. It affected the confidence of potential travellers, touching the most sensitive area of the travel business. If people do not have to travel to an area where there is perceived to be such a threat, they will not do so, even if the threat is small in real terms of probability.

As a consequence, the latter half of March and most of April and May 2003 saw drastic falls in tourism and travel activity throughout Asia and the Pacific. The region had escaped the worst of the 2001-02 downturn in international travel, but it saw its growth prospects destroyed by SARS. Typical estimates available in April 2003 included:

— a decline of one third in travel activity in March-April 2003 in the countries and areas directly affected-China, Singapore, Viet Nam and Taiwan, China;

— in Hong Kong, China, a growth of 19% in arrivals in the first half of March became a decline of 10% in the second half, with a 70% decline anticipated for April;

— a decline of perhaps 15% in the medium term in the rest of Asia and the main Pacific nations;

— a 30-40% drop in United States air bookings to the region, and almost a 30% drop in bookings on British Airways' Asian routes;

— 30% of flights to Hong Kong, China, cancelled;

— a 61% fall in arrivals in Singapore in the latter half of April;

— a 50% drop in arrivals in the Republic of Korea in April;

— hotel occupancy rates down to between 30% and single figures in some Asian destinations;

— predictions of a 40% decline in arrivals in Thailand for the April-June period;

Australian hotel occupancy rates down by 20-30%, with a 30% decline in tour operators' bookings for the destination in May and 20% in June. On 23 May the World Health Organisation lifted some of its advisories against travel to the region - 'freeing' Hong Kong, China, and Guangdong province of China among others. WHO's travel advisories against the other areas (Beijing, Hebei, Inner Mongolia, Shanxi, Tianjin and Taiwan, China) were lifted until 5 July. In most affected destinations, it is still too early to assess recovery measures, although in Hong Kong, China, the lifting of the WHO travel advisory has been used as an opportunity to re-launch the destination under the banner of 'Rediscover Hong Kong'.

The tourism authorities and the tourism industry were combining to generate positive messages about safety, coupled with the promotion of the destination by more traditional means such as special offers and price reductions. It is stressed that the recovery will take a considerable length of time and that the guard against SARS will need to be kept up, but the sector is also using well-recognised communications principles to deal with the situation in a professional manner.

The crisis illustrates the 'geographical blindness' on the part of many travellers, since there have been sharp declines in arrivals and in the level of business generally in countries within the region that have had no SARS cases. Even in other regions of the world, travel has been depressed as a result of the virus and of worries about how it might be spread through, for example, air travel. The fact that some such concerns may be scientifically ill-founded did nothing in the short-term to mitigate the effects. Based on past experience, it is likely that the tourism markets most affected will recover by 2004. However, there is no sign yet that the outbreak is fully under control. Until that point is reached, SARS seems to have caused serious damage to tourism demand, and thus to employment prospects, throughout the region.

Future Trends

The latest available formal forecasts of international travel to the Asia and Pacific regions are contained in Pacific Asia Tourism Forecasts, 2003-2005, published by the Pacific Asia Travel Association (PATA) in April 2003. These forecasts take into account the broad effects of the 2003 war in Iraq, but were completed before the outbreak of the Severe Acute Respiratory Syndrome (SARS) virus in March/April of 2003. Thus, it is likely that the impact of SARS will reduce travel demand in 2003 compared with the underlying trends shown.

The Pacific Asia Travel Association (PATA) forecasts predict that growth in international tourist arrivals for the period 2001- 2005 will average 5.6% a year, with very considerable variations between countries. As a destination, China was expected to grow most rapidly with Viet Nam also growing rapidly. Three countries - Indonesia, Nepal and Pakistan - are predicted to receive fewer visitors in 2005 than in 2001, while growth in two major destinations - Australia and Hong Kong, China - is predicted to be only nominal over the period.

The PATA forecasts for the first half of the decade until 2005 may be complemented with those produced by the World Tourism Organization (WTO) in 2000 under the title Tourism 2020 Vision. The latter were published before the events of 2001 and their repercussion in 2002, however, they were confirmed by WTO in general terms as recently as April 2003. Indeed they are meant as long term forecasts and tourism is expected to be back to high growth rates by 2005 if not earlier.

Regardless of possible differences in definition and methodology underlying each of the two data sets, the number of arrivals in the second half of the decade that would be needed to reach the WTO forecast implies annual growth rates in that period of has high as 20 per cent and more for certain countries. In order to reach the number of international arrivals forecasted by WTO for the end of the decade,(2010) starting from the base of the rather lean PATA forecasts for 2005, growth rates in the second half would have to achieve exceptional levels in some countries such as Indonesia or the Philippines.

The World Travel and Tourism Council (WTTC) estimates of employment in the tourism industry and in the tourism economy include medium-term projections to

2013. The WTTC forecasts for the next ten years show that total regional employment in the travel and tourism industry will rise by 21%, and in the travel and tourism economy by 25%. This would result in an absolute employment gain of over 28 million jobs, of which 8 million would be located in the travel and tourism industry directly.

The largest percentage gain in jobs in the industry is predicted to be in the small island states, in addition to which certain larger destinations such as Singapore, Malaysia and Cambodia will do well. A net loss of travel and tourism industry jobs is predicted only in Japan. In the travel and tourism economy, however, the greatest gains among the major destinations are predicted to be made in Malaysia and Singapore, and the small island states should also add proportionately large numbers of jobs. No loss of jobs is foreseen in any country. It is again interesting to note the separate positions of the two dominant economies of China and India. In India it is predicted that employment growth in the industry will be 14.1% and in the travel and tourism economy 16.1%; the corresponding figures for China are 14.7% and 21.1%. The position in the rest of the region is that much more rapid gains (of 34.3% and 35.2%) are expected.

For a more limited selection of countries it is possible to contrast the forecasted changes in international tourist arrivals with the forecasts for employment in both the travel and tourism industry and in the travel and tourism economy. For these countries - which are Australia, Cambodia, Indonesia, Republic of Korea, Japan, Malaysia, Philippines, Singapore, Thailand and Viet Nam - the WTO arrivals forecasts predict a growth of 68% in arrivals between the actual figures for

2001 and the forecast year of 2010. From the point of view of employment, the WTTC , forecasts that employment in the travel and tourism industry will rise by 29% and in the travel and tourism economy by 31%.

The implication, even allowing for the fact that the WTO arrivals forecasts may now look optimistic in the light of the depressed market conditions since 2001, is that productivity will rise in the industry, since the growth in jobs is predicted to be slower than the growth in international arrivals. It may be taken into account, however, that international arrivals are of limited use as an indicator for the total volume of travel and tourism business, as the duration of travellers' stay in the country and their consumption may vary as may the proportion between international arrivals and domestic tourism.

3

Asian Nature Tourism

Asian world tourism has grown from 21 million travellers in 1980 to over 58 million travellers in 1997. In 1996 East Asia and the Pacific generated 94 million arrivals world-wide. Approximately three-quarters of trips occurred within the region. The spectacular growth in Asia-Pacific travel is primarily due to the rising national prosperity, lower airfares, and increasingly liberal travel policies among these nations. Also, a number of the newly industrialised economies that are less apprehensive about their foreign exchange balances have relaxed international travel restrictions such as exchange rate controls, surcharges, and spending limitations. Much of the travel is multi-country and between the main cities of the region, and almost half the tourists take sponsored tours.

The growing middle class and retirees in Asia are using part of their increasing incomes and personal discretionary disposable free time to engage in overseas travel. They represent at least 73% of the increase in travel. Stimulated by economic recovery in Asia, world tourism grew by 3.2% in 1999, half a percentage point faster than in 1998. According to WTO Secretary-General Francesco Frangialli, after two years of decreasing tourist arrivals, East Asia and the Pacific bounced back strongly in 1999, reaching a growth rate of 7.5% and a new record total of nearly 94 million international tourists. This is nearly five million more tourists than the previous record set in 1996. Growth was widespread, with especially good results in Singapore (+11%) Japan (+9.6%), South Korea (+9.6%), Malaysia (+8%), China (+7.9%), Hong Kong SAR (+9%), and Thailand (+5.6%). According to WTO, all East Asia countries and jurisdictions except North Korea and Mongolia, ranked in world's top 40 tourism earners in terms of international tourism receipts. Inbound tourism to East Asia countries has certainly grown over the past two decades, with 10.3 million tourist arrivals in 1980, up to 31.9 million tourist arrivals in 1992.

In 1992, within the jurisdictions of East Asia, China led the way in both arrivals and average annual increase in arrivals. Hong Kong followed with the second highest, and South Korea with the third highest.In contrast to the well-developed inbound tourism market in most jurisdictions, the Asian outbound market is either at its introductory or growth stage, and rapid expansion is certain for many years to come, principally in the form of intra-regional travel.

There is a range of different natural areas in East Asia, from many cold alpine plateaus in the mountains, to tropical climates and coral reefs in the south. Some naturál areas, such as many coastlines and plains, are located amongst or near large human populations, while other areas, such as vast inland forests, steep mountains and tundra are remote and far from urban populations. A common element shared by many jurisdictions is the presence of extreme environments, such as jagged mountain peaks and busy ocean coastlines. Numerous environments and habitats are contained within the East Asia region. Many areas retain unique cultural traditions that date back thousands of years.

Special natural and cultural sites in East Asia have a long history rich in traditions, religious ceremonies and customs that captivate local people and international visitors alike. The East Asia jurisdictions (referring to countries, autonomous districts and other political entities) share a long and complex history, with each jurisdiction possessing a unique history, government and size.

In terms of area and population, China has the largest of both in East Asia. It is twice the size of Europe (excluding Russia's land area). China covers an area of over 9.5 million km^2. Its landscape includes divisions of forests, grasslands, deserts, plains, hilly lands and highlands and many mountains. China is the most populated nation in the world. At 1.24 billion people, it accounts for approximately 20% of the world's population. Roughly 80% of the population live in rural areas. Its enormous land and natural resources help it to be a rapidly growing industrial nation and urbanisation is widespread. Modernisation, urbanisation and communication have been attached to nearly every tourism destination around China, which is sometimes a problem with the tourism industry. Sustainable development is a key issue in such a process.

In contrast, the island of Taiwan covers only 36,000 km^2 with over 1,140 km of shoreline and a population of approximately 22.5 million. Rugged mountains can be found in the eastern two-thirds of the island, with flat to gently rolling plains in the west. Hong Kong is even smaller, covering 1,092 km^2, with nearly 7 million inhabitants. Despite its size and population density, approximately 40% of the natural landscape is protected. Scenic peaks and valleys lie close to the busy harbour and city areas.

Japan covers an area of 377,835 km^2 and consists of four main islands of volcanic origin. These four islands comprise 90% of the total area. The majority of the population inhabits only 3% of the country. More specifically, over 80% of the 126 million inhabitants live in highly urbanised areas along the coastal plains. The interior is mostly rugged and mountainous. In South Korea, 46 million people live in an area that covers 98,480 km^2. There are upwards of 3,000 islands of various sizes off the southern coast.

Covering 1.564 million km^2, Mongolia encompasses an area larger than Britain, France, Germany, and Italy combined. Unlike the other East Asia jurisdictions, it is entirely landlocked. With 2.3 million inhabitants, its population density (1.5 persons per km^2) is the lowest in Asia.

North Korea covers 120,540 km^2 and has a population of approximately 21 million people. Macau covers a small area of only 21 km^2 and has a population of 374,700 people.

In East Asia, the size of the jurisdictions, the landscapes and the populations vary immensely. Found within the rich and diverse geographical and cultural environments of the region are numerous unique tourism opportunities, including visits to parks and protected areas.

Tourism and East Asian Jurisdictions

Due to the large variety that exists within the East Asia jurisdictions, all protected area management plans must take into account many items distinct to the specific area in which each park is found. For example, the history of the area, the legal structure, the existing level of human impact on the natural environment, the proximity to human populations, and the distribution of human populations must all be taken into consideration when designing a management plan for a specific park or protected area.

The act of conserving nature and natural resources dates back to ancient times in many of the East Asia jurisdictions. Concepts of nature and nature protection are linked to ancient religious philosophies and practices of Confucianism, Taoism and Buddhism. Thousands of years ago, some of these cultures were aware of relationships between conservation and utilisation of natural resources and human survival. In China, the value of forests has been recorded for at least 2,500 years. Temple gardens, restricted hunting areas, and landscape forests created in the past have all contributed to species' protection. Even though the concept of nature protection has existed for centuries, the creation of modern day legislation and systems of legally protected areas has occurred within the last century. The small and densely populated country of Japan was the first to attempt to establish a modern day park system through official government legislation.

In 1873, Japan established ko-en (literally meaning public parks) which assigned government protection to places traditionally visited in spring at cherry-blossom time or in autumn to enjoy the autumn colours. A national parks law was passed in 1931, and twelve national parks were designated between 1934 and 1936. Conceptually, the process of establishing national parks in Japan paralleled Britain's.

Since land was largely privately owned, in order to establish national parks, the government created them where it recognised the need to preserve nature rather than limiting itself to areas of land owned by the state. Approximately 24% of the whole national park area (primarily in the western part of Japan and in the coastal areas) is privately owned.

The first nature reserves in China were declared in 1956. Since then, the area of protected land and the number of reserves have grown steadily, except during the Cultural Revolution from 1966 to 1976 when conservation practices were abandoned and protected areas were not protected. National nature reserves have significant international influence scientifically, and/or special value for scientific research, and local nature reserves are those other than the national ones which are representative and significant for scientific research. They can be managed by the local governments, autonomous regions or municipalities directly under the central government. A nature reserve consists of three parts: the core area, buffer zone and experimental zone. This is one example of park zoning used by the various jurisdictions in East Asia.

All of the park systems in East Asia use some form of zoning system that identifies varying levels of appropriate use and protection in different areas of the park or protected area. The protection and use of each area varies along a continuum, with strict protection and no human use at one extreme, and high human use and some infrastructure development at the other extreme. Between these two end points are varying degrees of use and development versus protection and conservation.

Threats of urbanisation as well as endorsement by the IUCN in the 1960s helped to establish Hong Kong's network of country parks over a three-year period in the mid-1970s. A total of 23 country parks (designated for the purposes of nature conservation, countryside recreation and education) and 15 special areas (areas with special interest and importance by reason of their flora, fauna, geological, cultural or archaeological features) have been established. Eleven of the special areas are located inside country parks.

Country parks and special areas cover a total area of over 400 km^2. The smallest one is less than two km^2. They are designated under the Country Parks Ordinance and managed by the Agriculture, Fisheries and Conservation Department of the Hong Kong government on the advice of the Country and Marine Parks Board. All the country parks have toilets, path-side maps and the larger ones also have visitor centres. Few countries have 10% of their land protected in parks and tourists often find them hard to reach. Yet in tiny Hong Kong, 40% of the land lies in its country parks and visitors can reach them easily.

Starting in the 1930s, three attempts were made to establish Taiwan's national park system. War in the Pacific in the 1930s and a lack of solid legislative support in the 1960s prevented the success of the first two attempts. In the early 1970s, support by a world-wide national park movement and the growing political influence of Taiwan's scholars and environmentalists helped to make the third attempt successful.

By the time the national park concept gained support, establishment of a national park system was a challenge since the island was already highly industrialised and densely populated. Large tracts of undeveloped land, traditionally used to form park systems in other countries, were not available. Fortunately, the remoteness of various mountain regions had left them in fairly pristine condition, and some mountain areas were designated as parks. Not wanting to limit the system to remote mountain areas, other national parks were also designated in areas already experiencing considerable, and sometimes incompatible land uses. In Mongolia, two nature reserves were established in 1957, and another six protected areas were established in 1965.

Until recently however, Mongolia's unique combination of diverse landscapes, unspoiled habitat and rare wild plant and animal species were unknown to most of the world. The Mongolian Law on Protected Areas was enacted in 1994, and during the 1990s there was a large increase in the numbers of designated areas in Mongolia. As major changes occur, the government is attempting to strengthen centuries-old traditional practices of nature conservation with modern approaches and resource management.

In the midst of great socioeconomic and political changes, the government established the Ministry of Nature and Environment, passed a series of environmental laws, and greatly extended the protected area system. Pressures for non-sustainable exploitation of the natural resources are increasing. Mongolia faces the challenge of developing the infrastructure and economy while at the same time protecting the natural environment.

South Korea has a long history of nature conservation, dating back over 1400 years. The first official national park in South Korea was established in 1967, and South Korea now has 20 national parks. The concept of national parks is a common occurrence in the realm of parks and protected areas. However, numerous other types of protected areas exist. In South Korea for example, protected area categories have expanded to include natural parks (divided into 20 national parks, 20 provincial parks and 29 county parks), nature forests, nature reserves, marine parks, ecosystem conservation areas, wildlife sanctuaries and wetland protected areas.

Various types of protected areas have different mechanisms for establishment, different purposes and varying levels of regulations, legislation and protection. Protected area legislation and laws vary from jurisdiction to jurisdiction in East Asia. Creating legislation that enables each jurisdiction to declare and protect natural areas of significance is a critical first important step in the development of a park system. Even though the specific details of legislation differ, the intent behind the legislation is common to all jurisdictions - legally to identify and protect a system of naturally and culturally significant areas. The on-the-ground creation of actual parks is the second step. It is equally important that an organisation charged with managing these areas be established and that it receive adequate political, social and financial support.

Jurisdictions in East Asia vary in the classification and titles of administrative systems as well as in the types of management organisations that look after parks and protected areas. Some are highly centralised and utilise a top-down approach. Others extend greater authority to regional management units. One challenge is to have cohesion and effective communication across the entire system of administrative agencies and ministries as well as within any particular agency between the headquarters and staff working at the ground level of a specific site. Even though government agencies that oversee protected area systems are not the same, some features are common to the various jurisdictions. For example, even though the term national parks is not always used, most of the jurisdictions have this type of protected area administered by a federal agency.

Often government park agencies are created and made responsible for managing park systems. Other agencies, such as non-profit organizations can also make valuable contributions to the management of park systems.

Tourism can be an effective vehicle in obtaining funds for the management of protected areas and for the well-being of communities surrounding these areas. Through tourism, the public can be educated about the importance of supporting the protection of these areas. Overall, tourism can be a key element in generating support for the protection of unique natural areas.

Protected areas, such as national parks, natural monuments or managed resource protection areas are legally protected through government legislation that officially designates these areas as protected. Other types of designations can also recognise an area's special natural or cultural significance. For example, countries can nominate areas to be accepted as internationally valuable through different conventions. Types of natural and cultural areas recognised at the international level include: World Heritage Sites, Biosphere Reserves and Ramsar Wetlands.

In recent years, one of the motivations for nations to nominate areas for internationally recognised designations of protected areas, such as the World Heritage Listing, has been a perceived link between this designation and the attraction of international tourists to the site. Once international recognition is granted, visitor numbers will increase. It is important to have a well-designed system of visitor management in place, along with methods of collecting some revenue from visitors to the world-renowned areas. It is possible to achieve a symbiosis between conservation and tourism. It is both desirable and feasible that some portion of funds generated by tourism to natural areas be reinvested in protection and management of those areas.

World Heritage Sites

A world heritage site is a natural or cultural site recognised by the international community as possessing universal value, and coming under a collective responsibility. A country nominates a site to the Convention, and a decision on whether to include it in the world heritage list is made by a 21-member international committee.

After a site is approved for inscription into the World Heritage List of Sites, the real work of preserving and conservation begins. There are 630 properties which the World Heritage Committee has inscribed on the World Heritage List (480 cultural, 128 natural and 22 mixed properties in 118 State Parties) current as of December 1999.

Biosphere Reserves

The Man and the Biosphere (MAB) Programme is an interdisciplinary research effort directed towards providing information for the solution of natural resources and environmental issues.

It is "an interdisciplinary programme of research and training intended to develop the basis, within the natural and the social sciences, for the rational use and conservation of the resources of the biosphere, and for the improvement of the global relationship between people and the environment". As an intergovernmental program, MAB presents an opportunity for international co-operation and a focus for the coordination of related programs aimed at improving the management of natural resources and the environment. There are 368 Biosphere reserves in 91 countries as of January 2000.

There are three zones of management in Biosphere Reserves: the core zone, the buffer zone and the outer transition area. The three zones are usually implemented in many different ways to accommodate local geographic conditions and constraints.

This flexibility allows for creativity and adaptability, and is one of the greatest strengths of the concept. National MAB Committees are responsible for preparing Biosphere Reserve nominations and for involving the appropriate government agencies, relevant institutions and local authorities in preparing the nomination.

Each nomination is examined by a UNESCO Advisory Committee for Biosphere Reserves, for recommendation to the International Coordinating Council of the MAB Programme. This Council takes a decision on nominations for designation, and the

Director-General of UNESCO notifies the State concerned of the decision. Once designated, the appropriate authorities are encouraged to publicise their Biosphere Reserves, for example with a commemorative plaque and distributing information material indicating this special status.

EABRN (East Asian Biosphere Reserve Network) is an example of a regional network. EABRN consists of China, North Korea, Japan, Mongolia, South Korea and the Russian Federation. This network, initiated in 1994, has three subjects as priority for co-operation: ecotourism, conservation policy and transboundary conservation. It also serves as a mechanism to facilitate an exchange of information, training opportunities and site-to-site co-operation.

On a national level, in 1993 China set up the first network of its kind (China biosphere reserve network) which consisted of 16 world biosphere reserves and 67 natural reserves located in China. Six meetings have been held so far, the last one in 1999 in the Jiuzhaigou Biosphere Reserve in China.

Ramsar Wetlands

The Convention on Wetlands, signed in Ramsar, Iran in 1971, is an intergovernmental treaty which provides the framework for national action and international co-operation for the conservation and wise use of wetlands and their resources. As of March 2000, there were 119 Contracting Parties to the Convention, with 1023 wetland sites, totalling 74.9 million hectares, designated for inclusion in the Ramsar List of Wetlands of International Importance.

Ramsar is the only global environmental treaty dealing with one specific type of ecosystem. The Convention's mission is "the conservation and wise use of wetlands by national action and international co-operation as a means to achieving sustainable development throughout the world".

The Ramsar Convention takes a broad approach in determining the wetlands that come under its protection. In general, wetlands are areas where water is the primary factor controlling the environment and the associated plant and animal life. They occur where the water table is at or near the surface of the land, or where the land is covered by shallow water. They are defined as "areas of marsh, fen, peatland or water, whether natural or artificial, permanent or temporary, with water that is static or flowing, fresh, brackish or salt, including areas of marine water the depth of which at low tide does not exceed six metres". They may also incorporate zones adjacent to the wetlands, and islands or bodies of marine water deeper than six metres at low tide lying within the wetlands. The coverage of the Convention extends to a wide variety of habitat types, including rivers and lakes, coastal lagoons, mangroves, peatlands, and even coral reefs.

China

Many Chinese communities in the jurisdictions of East Asia have ethnic ties with China. No travel or direct personal contact between these communities and their homeland was permitted for several decades. Only since tourism in China opened up in late 1970s has such travel been possible. The growth in ethnic Chinese tourism to

China has been rapid, to over 10 million arrivals in 1992, plus million excursionists from Hong Kong, Macau and Taiwan. With the incorporation of Hong Kong into China in 1997, and easier travel in and out of China, opportunities for ethnic tourism between China and countries with substantial Chinese communities remain high.

A large majority of international tourists China have ancestral ties. Tourism occurs mainly in the humid, highly-populated, eastern region of the country, where the majority of the large cities and historical attractions lie. Tourism in the western two-thirds of China is limited. There, the climate is more arid and the landscape is less suited for occupation. Infrastructure is therefore less developed, and the capabilities of supporting tourism are lower. It is also less appealing to the millions international visitors of Chinese ancestry since their ancestors are primarily located in the east.

In 1997 nation-wide statistics were tallied from 11,938 tourism enterprises. The major markets for China were Japan, Russia, South Korea and the United States. Chinese visitor counts are divided into numerous categories including compatriots, foreigners and overseas Chinese. Most measurements and analysis are done on the foreign component. Information about the purpose of travel and more detailed profiles on foreign visitors would be useful to collect. One estimate indicates that roughly 60% of visitor arrivals are for leisure, and 40% are for business.

China has been the most popular tourism destination in East Asia and the Pacific region from 1985 to 1999, with roughly 27 million arrivals in 1999. In 1999, China had the fifth highest number of arrivals worldwide, after France, Spain, United States, and Italy. International tourist arrivals grew from 1980, when 5.7 million tourists generated US$617 million, to roughly 63 million tourists in 1998, who generated $US12.6 billion. China is capable of playing an important role in the international travel industry. The strong growth of the gross domestic product (GDP), the increase in private consumption witnessed by China over the last years, and the loosening of travel restrictions on travel to and from China, all contribute to China's ability to exert a dominant influence in the region's travel and tourism scene. Based on WTO predictions, China is expected to be the top tourism destination in the world by the year 2020.

China's goal for the year 1995 was to double tourist receipts over that of 1991, and to redouble by 2000. From US$2.5 billion in 1991, the targets were for US$5 billion in 1995 and US$10 billion in 2000. Performance in 1992 showed good progress towards this target with receipts up 38.9% over 1991 to US$3.95 billion and arrivals up 28% to 6.33 million. The state approved plans to build 11 national holiday resorts, with incentives to attract foreign investors. This is part of the policy to transfer China's tourism from traditional sightseeing to the combination of sightseeing and holiday resort tourism.

Japan

From 1987 to 1992, continuous growth in tourism arrivals occurred, and visitor numbers reached an all time high of 3.53 million in 1991 (an increase of 50%). The main stimulus of growth was the Asian market (up 74.6%), notably South Korea (24.4%), Taiwan (18.6%), the United States (15.4%) and Hong Kong (4.4%). The three key markets are Taiwan (26.9%), South Korea (24%), and Hong Kong. Together they accounted for 72.5% of Asian arrivals and 47.4% of Japan's total inbound market in 1991.

Visitor arrivals to Japan increased steadily in the first three years of the 1990s, but by 1995, arrival numbers were lower than they had been since 1990. Major reasons for the decline in numbers were an earthquake in Kobe and the strong yen, which had a dampening effect on leisure arrivals. Only business travel remained strong. In 1996, with the weakened yen, interest in leisure travel was slightly revived, with some figures indicating an increase in total arrivals of approximately 15%. Despite this, the industry continued to suffer, with low margins and a changing, less lucrative market. The average length of stay in Japan had fallen, from 14.9 days in 1988 to 9.4 days in 1995. Tourism officials introduced a new strategy designed to revive interest in the country and have targeted a doubling of visitors to 7 million by 2005.

In terms of outbound tourism, in 1987 the Ten Million Program was launched, with the intention of doubling the number of Japanese travelling abroad to 10 million by 1991, a target which was reached a year early in 1990. After this success, the government of Japan formulated a new, wide-ranging action program called Two-Way Tourism 21.

Intra-regional Asian tourism and ecotourism were recognised as the two major trends of the 1990s, and efforts have been made to foster and assist the successful expansion of these two market developments. With the sharp influx of Asian visitors there is a shortage of qualified guides and interpreters. The Japan National

Tourist Organization (JNTO) has identified three areas to concentrate on for the future in order to promote inbound tourism. It plans to:

— expand its activities in the Asian market

— encourage efforts to attract visitors to Japan's regional area, and

— step up the promotion of Japan as a convention and exhibition destination.

Hong Kong

Tourist arrivals in Hong Kong have grown from under 2.3 million in 1980, to over 9 million in 1994. Hong Kong's role as a centre for regional trade, transport, tourism and services has been growing significantly in 1990s. This had a positive impact on the travel industry, which is the third largest earner of foreign exchange for Hong Kong. Tourism contributed HK$64 billion in 1994. The Hong Kong Tourist Association (HKTA) established a broad goal of receiving 10 million visitors, with receipts of HK$130- 140 billion in the year 2000. Hong Kong remains a major entry for foreign visitors to China, although it is no longer the major entry point.

Japan was Hong Kong's largest market source from 1971 until 1990, when Taiwan overtook Japan as the major market. Hong Kong has benefited from the sudden surge of outbound traffic from Taiwan. The surge is a result of rapid economic growth and the easing of travel restrictions. Hong Kong has benefited in two ways, both as a destination that appeals to travellers from Taiwan, and also as the major entry point for travellers from Taiwan into China.

Barred from travelling to China since 1949, it was not until October 1987 that Taiwan citizens were first allowed to travel to China via a third country such as Hong Kong.

In 1994 China became Hong Kong's largest market. Even though Japan is no longer the primary market, it is still very important financially, because Japanese travellers stay a little longer than Taiwanese travellers and spend substantially more. Japan also has the largest leisure percentage among Hong Kong's major markets.

The Hong Kong Tourist Association, a quasi-official organisation promoting tourism to the international clientele, has recently tried to encourage more visitors to take advantage of the country park system.

Taiwan

Taiwan is both a pleasure destination and a business destination in the Asia Pacific, and rapid growth of the industry is not foreseen. Visitor arrivals to Taiwan have grown from 14,068 in 1957, to 2,298,706 in 1998. Visitor expenditures in Taiwan have grown from US$527 million in 1977, to US$3.4 billion in 1997, an increase of 85%. Average daily expenditures per visitor have grown from US$72.43 in 1977, to US$193.56 in 1997, an increase of 63%. These numbers are impressive when examined alone, but in comparison to growth in other jurisdictions, the figure is low. In 1994 Taiwan had roughly the same number of visitor arrivals as India, and less than main regional destinations such as Australia, China, Hong Kong, Indonesia, Japan, South Korea, Singapore, and Thailand. Taiwan's largest tourism market is Asia-Pacific travellers, who account for over 70% of Taiwan's market.

Taiwan's inbound tourism market has been heavily dependent on just six countries, which accounted for 81% of the region's visitors from 1977 to 1994. Japan supplied the greatest number of visitors to Taiwan (45%), followed by Hong Kong (13%) and United States (12%). Also contributing were South Korea (4%), Malaysia (4%), and Singapore (3%). While these six jurisdictions have played a dominant role in Taiwan's tourism trade, Taiwan's attractiveness has expanded over time. In 1977 only 15% of visitors to Taiwan came from outside of these six countries, but by 1994 other countries accounted for 25%. Most of this gain by other countries resulted from Japan's decreasing importance to Taiwanese tourism. The number of Japanese tourists increased from 563,000 in 1977, to 824,000 in 1994, but based on percentage, the total visitors actually decreased by 12%, from 51% of the market in 1977 to 39% in 1994.

Growth in Taiwan's inbound market has been slow for most of the past decades. From 1997 to 1999 inbound arrivals have remained steady at roughly 2.4 million.

According to Fish and Waggle reasons for the low growth include:

— strengthening of Taiwan's currency in the late 1980s

— a shortage of new or strong international tourist/ leisure attractions

— tourist attractions not being readily accessible difficulties in obtaining appropriate travel documents, and a lack of direct air links between Taiwan and major tourist-generating countries.

The sharp appreciation of Taiwan's currency against most of the world's major currencies in the late 1980s made the destination more expensive for visitors. In recent years, the currency has become more stable, making this issue less significant.

South Korea

South Korea is situated between Asia's most sought after outbound markets, Japan and China. In addition, it is located only a few hours north of Taiwan's huge outbound market, and it is easily accessible from both Southeast Asia and North America. For the Southeast Asians, South Korea provides four distinct seasons, a novelty for residents of the tropics. As an airline hub, South Korea is comparatively cheaper than Japan and more technologically advanced than China.

In 1962 only 15,184 foreign tourists visited South Korea. Since then, tourist numbers have grown strongly, reaching 100,000 in 1968, 1 million in 1978, and 2 million in 1988. In 1998, there were over 4 million visitors. South Korea's strong growth in tourism arrivals in the 1970s and 1980s can be attributed to three stimulants.

First, the president created a series of five-year economic development plans that produced South Korea's "economic miracle" and brought increased numbers of foreign business travellers. Second, South Korea's normalisation of relations with Japan, its former colonial ruler from 1910 to 1945, helped the economy grow, and also attracted leisure travellers. Third, inbound tourism to South Korea consistently achieved double-digit growth during the second half of the 1980s due to the Asian Games in 1986 and the Seoul Olympics in 1988.

Tourists account for 72.1% of all arrivals to South Korea. In 1998 arrivals from Asia totalled 3.03 million, followed by 470,000 from the Americas, 380,000 from

Europe, and 40,000 from Australia and New Zealand. Japan is the primary inbound market, followed by visitors from the United States, Hong Kong and the Philippines. In 1998 tourists from Japan amounted to 1.95 million. A vast majority (96%) visited South Korea for sightseeing. Since the 1970s, Japan has been South Korea's major inbound market.

Japan once totalled as much as 70% of the total market, but from 1985 to 1995 it accounted for approximately 45%, with a temporary peak of 50% just after the Olympics. The decrease may be partially explained by the fact that a visit to South Korea became considerably more expensive in early 1990s due to increased costs of both labour and commodities. The tourism industry has made great effort to attract travellers from Japan. For example, the need for a Japanese visa was waived during Visit Korea Year 1994. This later became permanent.

The United States is the second-ranked inbound market for South Korea. In 1998 visitors from the United States totalled 406,000. The majority came as tourists. The average length of stay was 9.7 days, a relatively long period of visit. The United States has maintained strong links with South Korea since its participation in the Korean War from 1950 to 1953. There are still over 30,000 United States' military personnel stationed in South Korea, and at least that many more civilian workers and dependants.

The long-term Korean Promotion Plan, established in 1992 by the Tourism Policy Council, had a target of 7 million arrivals by the year 2000. Though previous marketing efforts have been concentrated on Japan, new efforts have also been made to diversify the market. The

Government's National Comprehensive Tourism Development Plan divides Korea into 24 tourist development areas and aims to spread tourism throughout the country. In 1994, total inbound tourism expenditures were US$3.8 million, and average expenditures per visitor totalled US$1.06.

According to the Ministry of Culture and Sports, there were 106,774 employees in South Korea's tourism industry. Jobs by sector include: accommodation (50,965 jobs), travel agencies (36,012 jobs), attractions (8,992 jobs), professional convention organisers (286 jobs) and miscellaneous (10,519 jobs). The Korean National Tourism Corporation (the national tourist office) is responsible for international tourism marketing, resort development, education and training, convention promotion, tourism research and development, and domestic tourism promotion. It provides licensing for tour guides (by language) and recorded 6,210 tour guides in 1995.

Mongolia

Landlocked between Russia and China, Mongolia became an independent republic in 1990 after 69 years of Russian influence.Since then, it has made a rapid transition from a centralised system to a market economy. For over 30 years, tourists have come to the Gobi Gurvansaikhan area,however, great changes in tourism have happened over the past decade. Recently Mongolia started to open its borders to foreign visitors. Until 1997 individual tourists to Mongolia needed formal letters of invitation from a Mongolian or a foreign resident to obtain visas. Since 1998 when liberal visa regulations became effective, there has been a noticeable increase in the number of individual tourists travelling to Mongolia. Mongolia's international tourist market has grown due to this policy. The Mongolian Embassy records list 200,000 visitors in 1995, of which 20,000 were tourists who generated an annual revenue of $6 to 7 million.

Improvements in visitor reporting are in progress, but some discrepancy in visitor numbers reported may still exist. Most recently, the Mongolian Tourism Centre reported 158,743 visitors in 1999, of which 34,049 were tourists who generated an annual revenue of $28.8 million. Based on Mongolia's relatively undisturbed landscape and culture, the potential for growth in Mongolia's nature-based tourism industry is large. Almost all leisure tourists visit Mongolia as part of an organised package tour. Some tourists choose to make independent travel arrangements. However, most tourists still need the services of tourism operators since travel in the countryside in Mongolia is extremely difficult without a rented car, an experienced driver or guide and an interpreter.

According to the Mongolian visitor arrival statistics of 1997, Japan is the single and most important tourism market in Mongolia (30% of the market). The majority of Mongolian package tours being offered in Japan feature an eight to nine-day itinerary. Mongolia is regarded as a special interest tour (SIT) destination for pursuits such as hunting and fossil digging, which appeal to a small and very limited market base. Western Europe is the second largest tourism market (with a combined share of 39% of the market). For most European tourists, Mongolia is a once-in-a-lifetime destination in Asia.

The tourist season in Mongolia lasts only five months of the year (May to September), with over 50% of leisure tourist arrivals concentrated in the months of July and August. One estimate identifies the number of tourism agencies at over three hundred in 1998. Among those 300 agencies, 100 companies are tourism entrepreneurs, of which 50 are general tourism operators and another 50 are travel agents. Until recently almost all of the tourism agencies have been based in Ulaanbaatar, and many of them manage campsites in the provinces.

Tourism in West Mongolia is in an early stage of development. Recently, international operators have started bringing a small number of tours to Mongolia, in co-operation with national tourism operators. Tourists interested in the nature and culture of Mongolia primarily come from industrialised countries such as Japan, Europe, Australia, North America and South Korea, and have high travelling budgets relative to the cost of living in Mongolia.

Tourism numbers to national parks are very small compared to other park systems in other East Asia jurisdictions. One estimate suggests there is less than 1,000 people per year who visit national parks in West Mongolia. It must be acknowledged that the reported tourist numbers in parks may not accurately capture all tourists - some do not register, either because they are not aware of the need to register, do not know where to go to register, or try to avoid paying the entrance fees at registration.

Although tourism in Mongolia is currently small scale, it will continue to play an increasingly important role in the region. Effective planning is critical in order to address the possible problems brought by increasing number of tourists. Mongolia government policy has been responsible for rapidly establishing a number of protected areas in the past few years.

Under the prerequisite of environmental preservation, tourism is regarded as a promising opportunity for Mongolia, with the ability to contribute to additional incomes by creating new jobs for the locals. Challenges to sustainable tourism development include poor accessibility to remote areas, lack of roads, uncontrolled flow of local people to areas of tourism development, insufficient tourism infrastructure and facilities in and around national parks and protected areas, and the inability for park budgets and staff to keep pace with the fast-expanding tourism industry.

Sustainable Tourism: Action Plan

A protected area management plan is the primary management tool to determine, publicise and implement objectives and priorities. All management plans should include a section on sustainable tourism management. Ideally, a national sustainable tourism strategy exists that will guide the development of strategies for individual protected areas. What works for one jurisdiction can rarely be applied without modifications to another ecological or socio-economic environment. However, there are strategic principles, common issues and consequential steps which are universally applicable to the development of management plans.

Table 1 is a checklist of all the major steps associated with creating a plan for sustainable tourism development within protected areas. Some items, such as creating an inventory of natural, cultural and tourism resources, are best placed in the early planning stages. If tourism development is already in progress without a plan, it is never too late to incorporate steps from the checklist in an attempt to better plan for development and associated impacts.

Table 1: A sustainable tourism action plan for protected areas

Item 1: State clear objectives for sustainable tourism for each park.

Item 2: Compile an inventory of natural and cultural features, as well as of existing tourism use and potential. Map and analyse the information.

Item 3: Involve local people. This is key.

Item 4: Work in partnership with local people, the tourism sector and other regional and local organisations.

Item 5: Utilise zoning to identify and plan for areas where higher levels of tourism impacts may occur without harming areas of ecological significance.

Item 6: Develop the limits of acceptable use for all parts of the protected area, set environmental standards, and ensure they are met.

Item 7: Determine which tourism activities are compatible with the protected area and which are not, and develop related policies.

Item 8: Assess the environmental, economic, social and cultural impacts of proposals for tourism development.

Item 9: Develop education and interpretation programs for visitors and local people that increase understanding and appreciation of the area's environment, culture, heritage and important issues.

Item 10: Design methods to channel visitors through desired areas with minimal negative impacts.

Item 11: Survey and analyse tourist markets and visitors' needs and expectations. Ideally, this occurs both before and after developing ideas for new forms of tourism.

Item 12: Brainstorm tourism products to be potentially developed and influence types of visitors choosing to visit. Identify the values and image of the protected area on which to base sustainable tourism and outline a promotional strategy for them.

Item 13: Establish a program for monitoring the protected area and its use by visitors. At appropriate intervals evaluate the success of the plan in ensuring that tourism use maintains environmental standards. Revise the plan as needed.

Item 14: Assess resource needs and sources, including provisions for training.

Item 15: Implement the plan.

It is neither necessary, nor desirable to implement items in the sustainable tourism action plan checklist in the sequential order in which they are listed. Determine a list of priorities that are best suited to the needs and current situation of the specific site to which they are being applied. Some items follow a logical discrete sequence, such as determining the limits of acceptable change before assessing new proposals for tourism development. Other items describe ongoing efforts, such as developing partnerships or involving local people in park planning and operations.

Objectives

ITEM 1: State clear objectives for sustainable tourism for each park. The first step in developing a sustainable tourism action plan is to identify the desirable objectives of sustainable tourism.

The overall goal of sustainable tourism within protected areas must be to conserve protected areas in the long term. This and other objectives should be discussed and agreed upon by the stakeholders of the protected area. Certain zones within protected areas will require stricter protection from visitors.

Sustainable tourism benefits the protected area, local communities, the tourism sector and the visitors to the area. Stakeholders can discuss and agree upon the ways in which they anticipate sustainable tourism will benefit the area.

Inventory of Assets

ITEM 2: Compile an inventory of natural and cultural features and of existing tourism use and potential. Map and analyse the information.

Performing inventories within a protected area traditionally refers to identification of flora and fauna species and the frequency and location of species' distribution. For ecosystem management to be based in science, adequate baseline information about the physical, geographical and biological characteristics, and existing and potential uses of the conservation area must be collected. This information guides planning and management of the area and can be used to develop public education programs.

By examining inventories of species (especially the identification of sensitive areas and endangered species) park managers can determine the best (and worst) areas for tourism activity and development. Strict protection and possible scientific study should be assigned to certain areas in which tourism is not appropriate or potentially highly destructive. This information is just one element necessary for developing an inventory for the purposes of sustainable tourism.

Information about current infrastructure and available resources is needed in order to plan and manage tourism in protected areas effectively. Planners and managers must examine natural resource data (such as location and frequency of species' distribution), as well as human structures, the context of the wider area, available resources and the existing infrastructure that will support tourism development. For example, regardless of the ideal location for a park entrance based on distribution of species, existing roads and infrastructure largely determine the location of access points, unless they can be blocked off and new ones can be afforded.

An interdisciplinary team should create a full inventory of the protected area and its surrounding peripheral or buffer zones. The inventory should be created through a partnership between park management staff, the tourism sector, and local communities.

Data analysis and identification of further necessary information are two important steps in this process. Protected area managers can apply data about the condition of natural and cultural features as they relate to visitor numbers in order to determine the limits of acceptable change of an area. Knowledge of visitor numbers, distribution, and activities will assist in the creation of effective visitor management measures to reduce negative human impacts on the protected area.

Good information systems and modern technology software are desirable for storage and analysis of the data. For example, GIS software (Geographical Information Systems) is practical for handling map-based data. Application of this software makes it possible to establish a GIS study on tourism and recreation that aims to identify and document the environmental effects of tourism on the park and its communities. Visitor surveys can identify visitor locations, patterns and trends inside the park and in the buffer landscape protection zone.

Alternative management options can be modelled through the computer program so that solutions can be found to issues such as traffic patterns and concentrations, location of toilets at campgrounds and vulnerability of vegetation in high use locations.

Local People

ITEM 3: Involve local people. This is key. A primary motive for supporting nature-based tourism is its potential to assist in nature conservation. This can only be successful if local communities obtain clear, sustainable and adequate benefits from the presence of tourism. The support of local people is key. Multiple-use planning will be more likely to succeed if the needs and desires of local, regional and international users are fully expressed and understood, and if local people are made part of the planning process. By enlisting their support, managers of protected areas make connections with people who are well informed, who are able to provide quality tourism services, and who may be the first and main point of contact visitors have in the area. Local people can be effective messengers for informing visitors about the history, culture, and special features associated with the protected area.

The conservation philosophy that has traditionally been used in the past in the creation of national parks has been a closed protection model. Parks were designed on the assumption that they were free from human influences. Large areas of land were set aside for protection. In non-populated areas, this system has advantages.

The challenge in East Asia is that in many potential locations where parks were to be designated, people were already living in some part of the area, and human influences were present. Using a traditional model, park agencies inform local communities of the specific park boundaries and tell them which activities are permitted and which are no longer permitted. Much attention is given to regulations and enforcement. In the traditional model very little consideration is given to the interests of communities in and around protected areas. Often no efforts are made to involve local people in the planning and management of the area, even though many regulations imposed by the park staff impact on the livelihoods of the residents. The results include poor relations between government park staff and local communities, confrontations, and lack of support for conservation activities.

One example of an alternative to the rigid conservation-focused traditional approach to protected areas is the biosphere reserve. Like national parks and other protected areas, one of their official functions is to protect genetic resources, the environment, the flora and fauna, etc.(conservation function). Biosphere reserves also have two other functions that address the human dimensions of park-human interactions. They are designed to facilitate sustainable development in socio-cultural, ecological and economic terms (development function) and to assist research, monitoring, environmental education and training, and information exchange related to issues on sustainable development at the regional, national and global levels (logistic support function). This is just one example where attempts are made to incorporate human considerations into the process of development and conservation.

All protected area systems need to incorporate human dimensions into their planning, management and decision-making processes. Ideally, in all park systems, local needs and concerns are listened to, and mechanisms for local involvement exist. Often this is not reality, and many problematic situations arise. This is especially true for parks that have been created without consideration for human influence in populated areas. Projects that do not take into account local interests and human resources, and that are imposed from the outside with no local involvement, usually do not support sustainable tourism development as a conservation tool.

When park agencies encourage involvement and try to gain support of local communities, the tourism sector and other local and regional organisations, they actively contribute towards the development of sustainable tourism in protected areas. Ideally, stakeholders are involved early in the planning process, however if planning and decision-making is already in progress, it is still never too late to facilitate local community involvement.

On an individual basis, local people can contribute valuable local knowledge when identifying opportunities and areas of concern. Problem solving discussions require their input. On a larger level, effective and capable local organisations and initiatives are worth the effort to develop and strengthen. Building the capacity of local agencies is more sustainable in the long term than getting foreign experts simply to do all the work to create a plan which gets left with local people who were uninvolved in the decision-making and planning processes. Without involvement in the planning process, there is no ownership to the plan. Capacity building of local people living in and around protected areas should be a focus of sustainable tourism development.

In situations where local control of tourism operations is possible, local communities will benefit more directly from tourism development in and around the protected area than where control is held by foreign investors or large organisations. Local control can help minimise negative social and cultural costs, and increase economic benefits. Local people will be more involved in decision-making, and a larger percentage of tourism spending will go directly to the local area. If park agencies retain a large degree of control, it is necessary to work at taking steps towards involving local communities in the management and decision-making processes. Various degrees of decision-making power need to be shared if the broader interests of local people are considered along with economic development goals.

Efforts must be made to secure consent and active support from local inhabitants in order for management of protected areas that overlap with communities and private land ownership to be successful. When local residents get benefits from reserves, they will become guardians of biodiversity conservation. Three ways to enhance benefits to local residents through ecosystem conservation include:

1. Admit property rights (ownership or right to use) of local residents to natural resources
2. Compensate local people for society-wide benefits arising from natural resource conservation
3. Encourage participation in conservation and management of the resources.

By involving the local communities in planning efforts, potential impacts on the natural, social and cultural environment are more likely to be considered from the perspective of the local communities.

Each community has different values and different priority issues. In one location cultural erosion may generate community opposition to tourism development. In another location environmental issues may be a primary concern. As well, communities vary in their ability and willingness to absorb and benefit from visitors. The plans and decisions are more likely be supported by local communities if they have been involved in the process and benefit from the decisions.

Partnerships

ITEM 4: Work in partnership with local people, the tourism sector and other regional and local organisations. Partnerships are the foundation for accomplishing environmental initiatives. This is a simple lesson to understand, but not necessarily an easy one to achieve. Much effort and commitment must be invested in order to form and maintain working partnerships. Partners can exchange skills in tourism, the environment and other disciplines. Examples of compatible organisations include conservation groups, research facilities, zoos, universities and museums.

Partnerships with non-governmental organisations contribute to effective planning and management of protected areas. Organisations can specialise in things such as the advocacy of natural area conservation or community development programs, or they can be general and broad based, covering a range of issues.

Examples of contributions made by non-government organisations include conveying to government ways in which management of a protected environment can be improved, educating communities on conservation principles, and developing voluntary guidelines.

If there is some hope that local people will be involved in the planning and management efforts, then they must acquire adequate skills. Sometimes training is beneficial and necessary. Partnership with outside companies can provide valuable opportunities for local people to gain experience and training. Training opportunities may be available for example, through international development aid programs. Partnering with outside agencies or organisations that are equipped to provide support enables local organisations to be developed and strengthened.

Existence of capable local organisations provides a structure though which permanent local involvement in planning and decision-making can occur.

A key element to achieving sustainable tourism development is finding a harmonious relationship between the place, the visitor and the host community. The objective is to avoid leaving the visitor feeling unsatisfied, exploiting the local community or depleting the resource.

Community-based partnerships help to conserve the special quality of a place, promote recreation opportunities and support the local community. Another example of what can be successfully achieved through working together is the establishment of new protected areas or the adjustment of boundaries on existing areas. Co-operation with other levels of government along with public consultation make such a large task possible

Extended achievements that are made possible through partnerships include working on joint projects and marketing, developing packages of complementary products, linking transportation networks and using economies of scale. For example, many small destinations can unite their promotional efforts and market themselves as part of a tourism circuit in order to attract more visitors overall to the area. Alone, any one of the individual small destinations might not be sufficient to convince a tourist to choose that location as a destination but if marketed together, they offer a broader variety of opportunities that will more strongly appeal to a larger group of potential visitors. Development costs can also be shared.

One example of creating linkages to market one destination with others is being considered in Xizang Autonomous Region. Efforts are planned to develop Lhasa, its capital, as a tourism centre which is linked to other destinations and attractions inside the region. As well efforts are planned to link with cross border tourism centres such as Nepal, whose strong ecotourism industry may provide an additional source of tourists. Despite the hard work and ongoing effort to establish and maintain partnerships, the results produced by partnerships are often worth the efforts required to build and maintain them.

Zoning

ITEM 5: Utilise zoning to identify and plan for areas where higher levels of tourism impacts may occur without harming areas of ecological significance. Zoning is an essential part of all protected area management plans. Its main purposes are to define and map the different levels of protection and use that will occur in the protected area and to separate potentially conflicting human activities. Zoning must be comprehensive, but also as simple as possible. This ensures it can be readily understood by the public and be translated into management actions and regulations that are easy to comply with and enforce. To avoid unnecessary regulation of human activities, each zone should have clear and justifiable objectives. Examples of zoning designations include areas of strict protection, low level use, intensive use, and park operations. If additions to park tourism infrastructure are necessary, a few items should be considered. Integrated management that addresses a range of threats and accommodates a range of stakeholder interests can be achieved through multiple-use zoning. Zoning forces planners and managers to think ahead and to quantify present and future social and environmental impacts.

Zoning determines the location of appropriate tourism development, including the construction of buildings and other facilities related to visitor management and park operations. When adding to park infrastructure, the following should be considered:

— Construct the minimum necessary

— Construct to aid visitor management (e.g., location and size of car parks)

— Structures should interfere as little as possible with the natural ecosystem

— Structures should not dominate their natural surroundings and should, where possible, reflect local traditions and local materials

— Environmentally friendly design should be applied to building design, construction and functioning.
— Consider waste minimisation and collection systems – energy saving should be encouraged, using renewable resources where possible, recycling waste water, and using natural filtration systems for sewage waste disposal
— Accommodation should be modest, comfortable and unpretentious.

Multiple-use zoning schemes can be used to minimise impacts on ecologically critical or sensitive areas. The design, nature and regulatory framework of a multiple-use protected area will depend on the primary objectives of the area. Zoning a protected area for multiple uses can ensure that critical core areas are not impacted. In some cases, environmentally or culturally sensitive sites may require special management but do not fit the existing zoning designations. Management plans should include the guidelines necessary for the protection and use of such sites.

Zoning practices should also extend beyond the boundaries of the protected area when possible and when necessary. For example, where visitor demand is high, more resilient areas outside the park boundaries can be developed to accommodate overspill, with alternative trail systems, picnic sites and information points.

Use Levels

ITEM 6: Develop the limits of acceptable use for all parts of the protected area, set environmental standards, and ensure they are met.

Limits of acceptable use

A concept that is fundamental to the management of sustainable tourism is the development of desirable limits of acceptable use. Simply stated, it measures the types and levels of use that are sustainable. Examples of questions to consider when determining these limits are "How much damage can the environment take?" and "How much degradation will be acceptable to tourists?" There is evidence that as environments become damaged or use levels and type changes, some tourists go elsewhere. Three types of limits are: a) environmental, b) cultural and social, and c) psychological.

— *Environmental carrying capacity* is the most traditional concept of the three. Environmental limits are assessed according to the "degree to which an ecosystem, habitat or landscape can accommodate the various impacts of tourism without damage being caused or without losing its 'sense of place'". The assigned limits may vary depending on the season. For example, wildlife is more sensitive at certain times of the year, such as during breeding season, and weather conditions and water levels can alter the ability for habitat to withstand the pressures placed upon it.

— *Cultural or social carrying capacity* refers to the "level beyond which tourism developments and visitor numbers adversely affect local communities and their ways of life." Tourism levels that are too high will interfere with local people's ability to go about their necessary daily routines, and after the initial curiosity and excitement associated with potential economic benefits fades, the local people may begin to resent tourists. Once communities become adversely affected, their ability to attract visitors declines.

— *Psychological carrying capacity* is the "level beyond which the essential qualities that people seek in the protected area (such as peace and quiet, few other people, few signs of human developments) would be damaged by tourism developments". Each visitor to a protected area has certain expectations, including approximately how many other visitors he or she expects to encounter. At a beach on a hot day a visitor can expect crowds of people, whereas on a backcountry hike a visitor will expect less people. Psychological carrying capacity addresses this expectation. When visitors' expectations are not met, visitors may leave feeling unsatisfied and unhappy with their experience.

Determining acceptable use levels

How many visitors are appropriate? In determining the answer to this question, planners and managers may consider setting different limits for different areas and determine whether or not current limits are realistic. The assignment of such limits is subjective and arbitrary. Therefore, the planning process used to determine the limits is critically important, more important than the numbers themselves.

Due to the highly complex nature of interrelations contained within the ecosystem, damage is sometimes difficult to discern until obvious degradation (e.g., erosion, vandalism or the disappearance of certain species) is already occurring. A habitat or cultural site may be permanently damaged, and even when restoration is possible, it is a difficult and expensive process. Therefore, when developing carrying capacities, it is wise to choose a more cautious approach, especially in sensitive areas.

One of the challenges in assessing carrying capacity is determining specific indicators that are outlined in a way that measurements can be made and limits can be established. Certain elements can be measured with a high degree of accuracy.

Other elements, especially those associated with the social environment, are much more difficult to measure. Any one site will possess many different factors, each with their own carrying capacities. Decisions sometimes become political ones, and immediate social and economic needs are positioned against longer-term environmental factors. Efforts must be made to consider both the short-term and long-term factors.

Controling visitor impacts

Problems associated with limits of acceptable use are frequently related to the behaviour of visitors rather than the actual visitor numbers. Most impacts are behaviourally dependent, not density dependent. Density issues are briefly outlined, and general strategies to control visitor impacts are discussed is crucial that an accurate assessment be made as to whether or not visitor density is the true primary problem, before steps are taken to reduce visitor numbers. Without this assessment, it is like applying a healing treatment to an injured area without accurately assessing what is wrong. The selected treatment may not be the best match and, therefore, not be entirely effective in addressing the problem. Would many negative impacts be reduced through encouraging changes in visitor behaviour regardless of a change in visitor density? After weighing these considerations, if is concluded that too many visitors are causing too much negative impact, different management options that address density concerns include: reducing visitor numbers in areas where numbers are too great limiting visitor numbers in areas before they reach critical or unacceptable levels changing the type of tourist travelling to the area. is also important to consider whether the goal of reducing visitor numbers is realistic. it even feasible to attempt to control or limit the numbers of visitors who arrive on the site? It is possible to control visitor numbers through pre-registration systems and effective marketing and promotions.

Since many negative visitor impacts are the result of visitors behaving in harmful ways, revising visitor behaviours is an important goal. Education of visitors, is a key element in getting visitors to change their behaviours. Visitor impacts can be controlled and reduced through various administrative and operational methods. These include zoning, user fees, schedules, activity regulation, infrastructure, quotas, visitor movement and access points. Each is outlined briefly.

— *Zoning:* Zoning is a fundamental management component that enables protected area managers to assign specific uses to specific geographical areas. In intensive use areas a decision may be made to "harden the site" and monitor impacts rather than try to control the number of visitors entering.

— *User fees*: It is usually necessary for park managers to charge sufficient fees to cover the costs of visitor management. However, charging user fees limits user numbers based on an ability to pay. Differential pricing policies are sometimes used.

— *Schedule of use*: Use can vary, for example through seasonal closure or assigned time intervals.

— *Activity regulation*: Some activities can be prohibited or restricted.

— *Infrastructure*: Infrastructure development controls how visitors use the site. For example, location and size of parking lots influence visitor use. The best and largest parking areas should be located within intensive use zones. Numbers of visitors and activities can be limited by the availability of lodgings, restaurants, tourism operators, etc.

— *Visitor movement*: Park visitors move through a park. The path a visitor takes can be influenced by the provision of clearly posted signs and trails. Education can increase visitor awareness of the importance and significance of species, and impacts, leading to care when travelling in park. Guides are often used to direct visitor movement. Physical structures can direct and control movement.

— *Access points, reception areas, gateways*: At entrance points park managers have the most control over visitor numbers, distribution and behaviour. Ideally when visitors arrive, they proceed immediately through a reception area where they can be met, have regulations explained, numbers counted, entrance fees collected and tours arranged. Information about the site should be provided. Information about the importance and need for visitor controls can also be explained. A well-designed entrance will ensure visitors have information about where to go, what to do and what not to do during the visit, and why it matters.

Setting standards

Once the limits of acceptable change have been assessed, the next step is to set standards based on people's use, understanding and valuation of the natural area. These standards are developed through input from technical and recreational park staff and discussion with all stakeholders. Once standards and management methods to maintain them are developed for the site, monitoring must be done in order to determine whether or not standards are achieved and maintained. The management agency, stakeholders and members of the public are responsible for monitoring and reporting on a regular basis how well the standards have been met. "This participative or co-operative management function enables those involved to modify standards or visitor use in response to actual ecological and social impacts".

Appropriate activities

ITEM 7: Determine which tourism activities are compatible with the protected area and which are not, and develop related policies.

Some recreational activities are acceptable, whereas others are not. It is critical that management policies are developed which outline the criteria used to evaluate the acceptability of activities. In general, acceptable activities are low impact, non-consumptive, promote education and awareness building, and fit with the goals and objectives of the protected area.

Appropriate activities often occur in small groups rather than large tours. Pursuits that require large infrastructure development, such as downhill skiing or involve motorised vehicles are examples activities that are usually not acceptable.

Major sporting events such as the Winter Olympics are not considered to be appropriate because of the scale and intensity of building and engineering work sensitive areas. Sports events focus on competition rather than the enjoyment of the natural area, and place unnecessary pressure on the protected area. Large, organised groups are often not appropriate in many zones of the protected area, and specific management interventions are necessary to prevent erosion of trails for example. Limitations should be stricter in Category II national parks than in other protected area landscapes where larger communities can absorb tourism development.

Most protected areas have legally enforceable regulations restricting the types of activities which are permitted.

Environmental, economic, social and cultural impact assessment

ITEM 8: Assess the environmental, economic, social and cultural impacts of proposals for tourism development. It is possible for sustainable tourism to play a positive role in the conservation of a protected area. As this concept gains acceptance among local businesses, the interest in capitalising on tourism opportunities rises. Proposals for tourism development increase. Private outside investors may be interested in capitalising on the protected area. International aid organisations may also want to get involved. Planners and managers need to combine their own vision for appropriate sustainable tourism development for the protected area with external demands for development. Tourists may also demand infrastructure development.

All tourism proposals need to be carefully assessed for their environmental, economic, social and cultural impacts. Environmental impact assessments are the most familiar assessment. One general question it addresses is how will the natural environment change based on tourism impacts? Social and cultural impact assessments are used less often, but they are also valuable. They combine objective (technical information) with subjective (political, social interaction, etc.) information in order to understand the opportunities and constraints presented by local communities to particular projects. Economic impacts are becoming increasingly common.

After doing an inventory and tabulation of the impacts, planners and managers must assess whether the identified and anticipated impacts are appropriate. It is critical that extensive public consultation be undertaken during the assessment and value determination.

Ecolabels can certify that specific, successful efforts have been made to apply concepts of sustainable tourism and reduce environmental impacts. Ecolabels can be a management tool used to improve the sector's sustainability (incorporating recognition, correction and monitoring of environmental impacts). Ecolabels are an important complement to regulatory tools, which should be designed to stimulate improvements that go beyond the regulations already in place.

Other environmental management tools include environmental auditing (a way of assessing the environmental damage caused by a business), environmental management systems (EMS offers a structured and systematic way of incorporating environmental considerations into all aspects of a business) and environmental reporting (a way of communicating environmental objectives, practices and achievements to stakeholders).

Education and interpretation

ITEM 9: Develop education and interpretation programs for visitors and local people that increase understanding and appreciation of the area's environment, culture, heritage and important issues.

Park managers play an important leadership role in environmental education.

Interpretation and public education programs promote the development of an environmental consciousness in the public and a willingness to take personal and collective action to protect and maintain the environment. Through interpretive programs, visitors can develop a better understanding and appreciation of the area's environment, culture and heritage, and the issues affecting it and the surrounding region. Through public education programs, and in co-operation with others, a stronger environmental ethic can be built, and support for conservation can be broadened.

Interpretive facilities, such as visitor centres, and publications, such as a brochure on the area, are designed with at least one of four purposes:

1. To increase visitors' awareness about a resource or attraction (e.g., local legends, history, unique

landmarks and sites). This gives visitors an idea of what life in the community is actually like.

2. To alter the behaviour patterns of visitors and residents. Explain why certain things should or should not be done, rather than just telling people not to do it. For example, a sign saying "Stay off the trail" only makes people more curious about what is on the trail, versus a sign saying "Overuse of this trail has caused erosion - Help nature rebuild it by choosing another route".

3. To explain community, organisation, or agency goals and objectives to visitors and residents. This not only increases awareness of their purpose, but also fosters community support of them.

4. To orient visitors to the area. Providing a list of different attractions and resources and directions on how to get there, helps visitors identify which they are interested in seeing and simplifies travel routes during their visits.

Properly planned and designed interpretive programs relay a theme and a message to visitors. A theme is a concept, idea, or message that visitors take away with them. A major program theme should relay a message or concept. Topics relay information related to the theme. Themes incorporate three learning components:

1. *Educational component* - What information do you want people to learn?

2. *Emotional component* - How do you want them to feel after experiencing it?

3. *Behavioural component* - What actions do you want to suggest they take?

For example, an interpretive sign to keep visitors out of a fragile wetland area would explain impacts of visitor use on the area (educational), how this harms flora and fauna of the area (emotional), and how visitors can prevent this impact by staying on boardwalks (behavioural).

Educating tourists through interpretation programs is a desirable goal. Education can also be applied to local people. Laws perform a necessary function of prohibiting improper and damaging use of protected area resources. Sometimes local people who have used the land and its resources long before the area attained protected status resent being told to act differently and do not understand the larger situation. In this case, laws will not resolve the fundamental problem of attitude and motivation. These issues are best addressed through education. Whereas law enforcement externally motivates people to change their illegal behaviours, education internally motivates a long-term sustainable change in behaviour. Once people understand the significance and special nature of the resources, they are more likely to accept the rules that exist to protect the area. When local people recognise the value of their environment, stewardship and a vested interest in conservation and sustainability can ensure long-term effectiveness. Designing well-planned tourism, ensuring income is distributed to local people and fostering a sense of pride in the environment are ways to encourage local people understand the full value of their environment.

Visitor channelling

ITEM 10: Design methods to channel visitors through desired areas with minimal negative impacts. Examples of questions that planners and managers should consider when designing channels for visitor movement throughout the park include:

— How do visitors arrive? (e.g., cars, buses, walking, bicycles)

— How should visitors arrive? Is it better to maintain the current methods of arrival or to encourage alternative forms of transport?

— Where do they arrive now? Do they arrive in sensitive areas? How do concentration points fit with the zoning scheme? Are existing movement patterns accommodated in the zoning scheme?

— Where should visitors arrive? Are there possible access points in or near intensive use zones? How many access points are most desirable (e.g., one or more than one)? How will points of access be controlled?

— Where should visitors go after they arrive? Ideally, visitors will be directed to the different use zones that have been prescribed in the plan, and will correspond to predicted numbers and frequency. Does the zoning plan acknowledge traditional use areas and distribution patterns and any desired changes?

— How will visitors reach these areas?

— Walk on trails?

— Is vehicle access permitted?

— How do people travel in the area now?

— What kinds of experiences are available or desirable for visitors to have?

Different levels of experience can be offered to visitors, from large-group tours, to wilderness adventures in small controlled groups. What types of accommodations are available? Are trails self-guided or accompanied by a guide? Decisions are guided by the zoning plan, tourist markets being targeted, and available resources.

Shuttle buses

Shuttle buses can be an effective way of regulating entry and distribution of visitors. They can also be an attraction in their own right. The park agency can control how often they are run (e.g., one per hour or on demand). Resources considerations include sufficient parking space, back-up transportation if a shuttle breaks down and maintenance, safety and insurance requirements.

Trails

The location and destination of the trails largely determines the on-site distribution of visitors. Trails should be carefully planned. They can offer different levels of experience and duration, and should be accessible from the main access point.

Well-designed trails will:

— be easy to find take visitors to interesting or well-known features

— accommodate a range of walking abilities (e.g., short, moderate, long, difficult, and easy)

— be easier to walk on than surrounding land

— be contoured on hills

— encourage a one-way flow of traffic (e.g., loop trails)
— have direction indicators at crossing points and in confusing sections of trails avoid very sensitive habitat types or species.

Self-guided trails that visitors navigate themselves are usually located in intensive use zones. Trail guides and good, easy-to-read maps are critical. Park staff or private tourism company guides may be desirable for larger groups and for travel into more sensitive areas. Park staff should be available for information provision, enforcement and monitoring.

Bookings, information and promotion

Some sites only allow visitors to enter if they have pre-booked their visit. For this method to work the park needs to be able to control access and enforce the need for pre-bookings. Information needs to be provided to visitors before they decide to visit, which can be accomplished by creating good links with tourist information centers, hotels and tourism operators.

Registration

Registration at the point of entry provides a means for monitoring visitor numbers, activities and types (e.g., nationality, age range, group size, etc.).One example where conscious efforts are being made to channel visitors through the area via two designated routes is at Changli Golden Beach Reserve in China. One land route and one water route have been designed to encourage visitation to certain areas (i.e., to spread out the high concentration of visitors in over-used areas) and to keep visitor traffic away from other areas (i.e., with the aim of reducing the negative impacts to the environment). A second example of innovative visitor channelling is at Jiuzhaigou Nature Reserve in China. Air pollution from cars and terrible traffic congestion inspired a creative solution to develop an environmentally friendly public transport system to take visitors to and from the various scenic spots inside the reserve. Each public car has a trained interpreter who describes the value of the scenery and unique characteristics of each scenic spot. The green environmental car service helps to protect the natural environment, enhance mobility of visitors and improve traffic order. This management program is part of a well-designed attempt to take an active role in protection, education and co-operation with others.

Market Research

ITEM 11: Survey and analyse tourist markets and visitors' needs and expectations. Ideally this occurs both before and after developing ideas for new forms of tourism. Protected area managers must do market research in order to understand their visitor profiles. Examples of relevant questions that should be asked by planners and managers include:

— Who are the visitors, and what are their characteristics?

— Where do they come from, and how did they get here?

— What percentage of visitors are local, domestic and international?

— How long do they stay?

— How many visitors are currently attending the site?

— What do they do during their stay?

— What attitudes and expectations do they have?

— What would visitors like to see?

— What motivated them to choose a specific protected area as their destination?

— How satisfied are they with their visit?

Learning about and analysing visitor needs and expectations better enables park managers to provide satisfying experiences that will meet visitor needs and expectations. Focusing on specific market segments enables park managers to target visitor services more effectively. It is also worth noting that although sometimes visitors may express a certain desire for a particular experience, this demand may not be true to the area's image. For example, visitors may express a desire for luxurious accommodations within the protected area in order to wake up to a breath-taking view. However, developing this type of infrastructure may be inappropriate, depending on the goals of the protected area and on the proposed location. It is important to decide what the specific area's ability is to meet demands of tourists. It is acceptable to declare a market demand as infeasible to implement, in light of protection or the non-sustainable nature of a proposal.

Visitor profiles can reveal important information to the manager. Information should be collected for various visitor groups. One group that is often ignored is the non-visitor. However, this group can also provide valuable information. Who is not visiting and why? Potential tourism markets can be identified through this line of questioning. If park managers want to expand to different markets, this type of questioning is very useful as a means of identifying potential tourism markets. It can also identify types of changes that may need to occur in order to attract these potential visitors.

Through interactions with visitors and also through partnership with social scientific research, park managers can identify components of satisfaction of the experience, what expectations visitor hold, how their expectations can be developed, and decide whether their expectations are realistic. Simple marketing research is very useful for a tourism development plan. As well as considering the present condition, it is important to anticipate future conditions.

Travel companies that design and coordinate trips and tour operators and guides who control activities in the destination should share a conservation ethic. Interactions between thesestakeholders and park staff enable information to be shared and a common understanding of one another's goals to be developed. Park managers should make the effort to educate these stakeholders on the importance of conservation and to outline the goals and appropriate activities for different types of parks within the jurisdiction. The shared ethic of conservation provides the framework within which all marketing and travelling efforts take place.

By making the effort to educate these stakeholders who are involved in the early planning stages of tourists' trips, planners and managers are actively influencing the types and expectations of visitors to the site. As a result, this reduces the level of on-site damage control efforts related to visitor management issues such as dealing with visitor conflicts, inappropriate behaviours and dissatisfied visitors. Two marketable aspects of a destination are attractiveness to travellers and the tourism infrastructure Marketing, advertising and communications should be designed to appeal to specific, desired target markets. Visitors can be segmented based upon demographic, psychographic and geographic characteristics. Park managers must identify anticipated characteristics of specific visitor groups in order to target these potential visitors with programs and services that correspond to their interests.

Identifying the types of activities that park visitors like enables planners and managers also to identify appropriate sources of advertising. Magazines and journals may be a good place to advertise. For example, many nature tourists are amateur photographers, so photography publications are a potential source. Specialised magazines, some of which are affiliated with internationally recognised organisations, are a prime source of advertising. Upscale travel magazines and special travel supplements in newspapers are other sources. Planners and managers can collaborate with tourism operators to develop brochures. Travel brochures should indicate the purpose and uniqueness of the destination. Promotions can generate consumer excitement and expand the message of sustainable nature tourism to a wider audience.

Product Development and Promotional Strategy

ITEM 12: Brainstorm tourism products to be potentially developed and influence types of visitors choosing to visit. Identify the values and image of the protected area on which to base sustainable tourism and outline a promotional strategy for them.

Marketing and product development are commonly used terms for activities in advertising and private industry. Since protected area management focuses on conservation of natural and cultural resources, advertising terms and activities used by private industry are likely unfamiliar territory to protected area managers. Developing a sustainable tourism action plan through multi-disciplinary partnerships will enable park managers to gain an appreciation of the role that these non-traditional park terms and activities can play within protected area management by developing multi-disciplinary partnerships with organisations more familiar with such terms.

Since many tourists want a varied experience, there are good opportunities for partnerships in marketing. Product linkages can be extended into marketing linkages. A key strategy is to develop a marketing mix that is attractive. For example, instead of promoting marine tourism all by itself, marine tourism in the area can be linked to culture, recreation, nature, wildlife viewing, etc.

Sustainable tourism development needs to be market based, focusing on the image and special qualities of the specific protected area, and targeting tourism markets which will be interested in buying these products. Protected area managers are thus able to have a greater influence over the types of visitors who come to the protected area, than through implementation of the market-led approach (developed according to demands of the market). In this way, managers can encourage individuals who possess characteristics that support conservation efforts, who wish to participate in appropriate activities, and who want to learn about the areas special features, to come to the park.

Many visitors have a keen interest in learning about what features make the area significant and unique. Park managers should explore opportunities to develop tourism products that take advantage of educational aspects. Once visitors gain a deeper understanding of the area's significance, they will be more likely to support its protection. Park managers can also discourage visitors whose behaviour or interests do not correspond to park goals. Consumers are concerned about the environment, and will likely ask questions. Basic interpretation facilities are a valuable tool through which common questions can be addressed. To address more complex questions from highly-educated visitors one option is to establish partnerships with compatible organisations such as conservation groups, research facilities, zoos, universities and museums who may be interested in developing programs that provide specialised information.

Protected area managers should brainstorm ideas and proposals to create various educational programs, themes for park tours, trail development, etc. that are appropriate to the area's objectives and resources. Managers should keep in mind the inventory of park assets and facilities, along with facilities and assets of the surrounding communities when developing ideas. Proposals for new developments in and near protected areas may be based in commercial development. Before permitting development, planners and managers should carefully examine a variety of relevant factors, including whether the development will result in excess use, and whether the use is appropriate. An analysis of the proposal for commercial development should be shared with appropriate planning and legislative agencies. In appropriate cases an environmental impact statement should be prepared.

Reference should be made back to the inventory of tourism and infrastructure resources. In terms of product development, what opportunities to develop tourism products and businesses exist? What opportunities should be encouraged to thrive? In terms of promotion, park managers should be aware of the types of expectations that visitors possess. Many travellers have come to expect a certain standard of comfort on a holiday (e.g., a level of quality of restaurants and hotels), and many people desire to see spectacular views with as little effort expended as necessary.

Formation of expectations occurs through images and messages presented through advertising, which is why protected areas and tourist organisations should be careful about what images are portrayed when promoting tourism of protected areas. For example, promoting the natural beauty or spectacular wildlife of the area while at the same time also promoting easy access and high standards of accommodations and entertainment may cause conflict and unrealistic tourist expectations.

If easy access and high standards of tourism infrastructure are not permitted in a sensitive protected area, then advertising must provide realistic images so that appropriate tourist expectations can be developed. Parks Canada has now established a visitor satisfaction goal for each national park and each national historic park in Canada. This is the first time that a park management agency has set specific targets for client satisfaction. It is important that both protected areas and tourist organisations work to portray the protected area destination accurately, both in terms of the special natural and cultural features it possesses, as well as in terms of the realistic limitations associated with conserving its naturalness.

Images should reflect the true value of the area, promoting a message of visiting nature on its terms, rather than massively altering the landscape to provide deluxe facilities that are insensitive to the primary attraction - the natural environment. Good standards of tourist services can be provided near protected areas but they should incorporate good sustainable design principles, including harmonising with the local environment. "Much of the infrastructure normally associated with 'mass' or package tourism is not compatible with beautiful views, undisturbed nature and the peace and quiet of protected areas".

One example of an appropriate message that could be conveyed through promotional images of protected areas is that breath-taking scenery and glimpses of wildlife will only be fully revealed to visitors who take the time to integrate themselves into the natural environment and experience its glory. These types of visitors will want to participate in low-impact activities. This message might discourage visitors who want to rush through it in a hurry to complete their checklist of stopovers. Their activities may be more consumptive in nature.

Quiet, low-impact activities, compatible with values supported by protected areas, are desirable and should be encouraged, especially in promotional materials. If images convey only activities that are compatible with sustainable tourism, visitors who desire more undisciplined and unruly activities may choose to travel elsewhere. If accurate images that portray the underlying values supported by protected areas are developed, self selection of visitors will enable management to avoid potential negative impacts caused by certain types of visitors.

Monitoring

ITEM 13: Establish a program for monitoring the protected area and its use by visitors. At appropriate intervals evaluate the success of the plan in ensuring that tourism use maintains environmental standards. Revise the plan as needed.

Monitoring is required to detect changes over time through comparison of two points in time, and determines whether these changes are due to natural causes or to stress caused by human activities. Monitoring visitor impacts enables park managers to assess whether visitors are causing unacceptable levels of impact and whether management controls are effective and sufficient.

Incorporate links to scientific research

Managers of protected areas can work closely with universities to create an ongoing research portfolio. Results of studies that examine environmental impacts of tourist use can be compared to inventory information recorded in the early planning and development stages (benchmark information). If a preliminary inventory has not yet been recorded, then this must be made a priority, and completed. When seeking partnerships with research institutions, protected area planners and managers may logically and intuitively focus on the collection of environmental data (since it is often the physical natural environment of which they are in charge of protecting). However, it is equally important to collect data on social, cultural and economic impacts of tourism. Examples of the types of social and cultural questions that research studies can address include:

— How should nature conservation benefit from commercial activities of nature tourism?

— How does tourism development in the area contribute to social and economic well-being of local communities?

— What skills are necessary for local people to participate in a community-based nature tourism project?

— What factors may prevent the success of such projects?

Develop indicators

Planners and managers must choose indicators of change. Indicators are dependent on site objectives. Is the site's primary interest natural, archaeological, cultural, historical, etc.? For example, if the site's primary interest is natural, then many monitoring parameters will relate to its ecology. These are linked to ecological carrying capacity. Other indicators, linked to social and cultural, and psychological carrying capacities should also be considered. Common environmental indicators include:

— *Loss and/or change in the vegetation structure*: Vegetation is easily affected by people or vehicles travelling over it. A simple way to monitor changes is through fixed point photography. Sample areas can be chosen with common sense. They should be comprised of highly visited and less visited areas of the same vegetation community.

— *Trail width and depth*: The amount to which trails get wider and deeper reflect visitor pressure. Proper design and good positioning can minimise deterioration. If trails become difficult to walk on, visitors may travel on undisturbed areas. Sample sections near the beginning, middle and ends of trails can be measured for width, depth and profile to monitor changes. Sometimes serious degradation in high use areas where trails have not be effectively designed is highly noticeable, even without scientific measurements.

— *Hot spots*: Changes to areas where visitors congregate should also be monitored.

— *Disturbance to animals*: This is more difficult to monitor, since animals are not stationary. One method is to perform annual counts of target animals, however this is time consuming and expensive. Feeding and nesting areas, especially of endangered species, should be avoided or have strict use limits so that disturbance is minimised.

— *Visitor control*: One indication of ineffective visitor control is the number of people found in sensitive areas. Park staff could record visitors seen in off-limit areas, walking off trails, attempting to enter illegally, etc.

Through development of a monitoring program, it is possible to identify the various steps and decisions associated with different development projects, and to note their contribution to successful protection or degradation.

Monitoring is time consuming and is neglected by some organisations. For monitoring to work over the long term, some of the techniques should be simple, inexpensive, easy to repeat with non-specialists, and if possible, should become part of the routine work of site staff.

Resources and Training

ITEM 14: Assess resource needs and sources, including provisions for training. Management plans should indicate staffing needs and identify major functions.

Volunteers, consultants, and head office staff involved in the planning process should also be identified as this will provide a more accurate indication of staffing levels. Incorporation of this step allows deficiencies to be predicted and recommendations suggested. All protected areas require staff with specialised training in visitor and tourism management. The staff functions are many.

The tourism competencies that must be present within a protected area management agency are:

1. Understanding visitors' needs and wants
2. Service quality management
3. Leisure pricing policy
4. Leisure marketing
5. Tourism and resource economics
6. Finance
7. Tourism management
8. Interpretation.

It is important that the park agency hires people with these skills, or encourages existing personnel to gain education in these fields. It is also important that all park staff receive training in how to react to accidents and other emergency situations. Visitor safety, accidents, liability and search and rescue are issues that must be considered by park tourism managers.

1. Understanding visitors' needs and wants

2. *Service quality management*: It is critical that visitor services are provided at the highest standard of service possible. Some park agencies have developed service quality goals, into their management goals. One example of a service quality goal is to have the majority of the visitors feeling that they received excellent service levels.

3. *Leisure pricing policies*: Most sites charge admission. Therefore, there must be a policy that determines the levels of prices. Many questions must be addressed. Are fees to be charged per person or per group? Are there different fees for different stakeholders or user groups? Are there different fees according to times of the day or seasons of the year? One example of differential pricing is to charge higher fees for higher levels of visitor services. Park planners and managers should develop a policy on fee collection.

4. *Leisure marketing*: It is important that park tourism managers understand the market for their services. What are the potential park visitors looking for? When do they want to visit? What services do they want to find at the site? How much are they willing and able to pay? These and many more key questions must be addressed in a marketing plan.

5. *Tourism and resource economics:* Tourism is often a primary revenue source for the local economy and the country. At the national level, government needs to be convinced that tourism will supply a significant amount of foreign exchange in order for them to provide technical and financial support for the protection of parks and protected areas. Actions must also be initiated and sustained through continuous

investments until conservation objectives are met. Governments alone are not able to provide funds for protected area operations. Financing conservation efforts requires mixed strategies involving a combination of approaches and partnerships. Examples include grants and loans, user fees, development of public/private partnerships and community-based, co-management arrangements that build on local incentives.

6. *Finance*: Sufficient finance to cover park management is a universal issue. All parks need money. Development and implementation of management plans, interpretation, education, training, research, monitoring, and enforcement programs all require financial resources. Often these funds come from general government tax revenues. However, in recent years, the creation of new parks and protected areas has outpaced the ability of governments to pay for management. Many park agencies have developed finance structures that allow a more business-like approach to park management. Simply stated, these new management models encourage park agencies to function like a private corporation. Key components include:

   — all revenue stays with the agency

   — multi-year carry over of budget

   — flexibility in pricing policy

   — a flat management structure

   — flexibility in the application of licences and contracts for concessions

   — innovation in service delivery

— a visitor-focused administration

— flexibility in staff reward, including incentives for good practice

— high levels of private - public coordination, and

— staff with visitor management expertise.

Parks Canada is one agency whose management structure has been redesigned so that they now utilise some of these components. Importantly, the vast majority of the income for this new approach comes from park visitors and park tourism. For example, costs of operating visitor services can be paid for by through park visitor fees.

The potential sources of income from park visitors include:

— Park Entrance Fees

— Recreation Service Fees, Special Events and Special Services

— Accommodation

— Equipment Rental

— Food Sales

— Parking

— Merchandise Sales

— Licensing of Intellectual Property

— Cross Product Marketing.

It is critical that park staff have good levels of understanding of park and tourism finance. All plan implementation must be monitored, to see if the policies are being successful. If problems are found, the implementation procedures must be alerted or the goals must be changed.

7. *Tourism Management*: It is important for park agencies to have specialised expertise in the planning and management of tourism.
8. *Interpretation*: One of the most visible tourism competencies is that of interpretation. Most successful guide training programs share a number of characteristics.

Implementation

ITEM 15: The sustainable tourism action plan should be implemented. Later, adjustments may be made based on monitoring and project results. Publicising successful projects so that others may learn valuable management lessons from others' experiences is useful. It is very important the park tourism plan be part of the overall management plan for the entire site. Tourism must be considered along with resource management, personnel management, public relations and all of the other important issues that are addressed in a park management plan. A balance must be found between planning, implementation and evaluation.

Does a protected area achieve its management objectives (including tourism objectives)? A common reason that protected areas do not achieve management objectives is because resources outlined in the planning phase exceed the amounts that are actually available for implementation. Even less attention is given to evaluation of success of management. In order for protected areas to achieve their management goals, once the management plan has been implemented, it is essential that monitoring and review occur regularly. Monitoring and review should be part of all management programs. Sufficient financial, technical and human resources must be provided over a timeframe that is long enough to allow for effective creation, implementation, monitoring and review of management plans.

4

Trends in Park Tourism

Nature-based tourism is the travel and tourism activity dependent upon the destination attributes of the natural environment. It dependent upon two fundamental components:

1) appropriate levels of environment quality and
2) suitable levels of consumer service.

Nature-based tourism has become sufficiently large that submarkets are becoming apparent. Ecotourism involves travel for the discovery of and learning about wild, natural environments.m Wilderness travel involves personal re-creation through primitive travel in natural environments that are devoid of human disturbance. Adventure travel is personal accomplishment through the thrills of dominating dangerous environments. Car camping is safe, family travel in the interface between the wild and the civilized. This classification utilizes unique sets of social motives to identify the market segments. Each of the niche markets is at a different stage in the typical business cycle using tourism life cycle analysis.

Ecotourism and adventure tourism have considerable growth potential, according to this analysis.

Wilderness travel is reaching capacity in many locales because of the requirement of very low-density level use in wilderness destinations. Car camping is probably in decline, or soon will be, largely due to the peak population profile of the developed word passing beyond the ages in which camping is popular. All four of these market segments are visible in park tourism internationally. Given the different travel motivation sets in each submarket, it is important for planners and managers to be aware of the implications for park visitor management. For example, the levels of social grouping, the level of desired service, the level of environmental quality and the desired environmental attributes vary amongst the four submarkets.

Nature-based tourism is a large and growing component of international tourism. Several countries in the world have nature based tourism as a key component of their most important export industry, tourism. These countries include Australia, Kenya, Nepal, New Zealand, Tanzania, Costa Rica, and Botswana; to name a few. Any one country has global competition in this field and this competition is becoming more sophisticated each year. The economic importance of the tourism industries in these countries is leading to more thoughtful policy and institut ional development. It is important to recognize the constructive role that can be played by positive and consultative policy development in nature-based and park tourism. Three examples are worthy of note, Australia, Tanzania and New Zealand. The national ecotourism strategy for Australia succinctly summarizes the background to the aggressive and successful policy development in that country: ecotourism offers the potential to generate foreign exchange earnings, employment, and other economic and social benefits, particularly in regional areas. It presents Australia with the opportunity to make the most of its competitive advantage, with its spectacular and diverse natural features, unique flora and fauna and diverse cultural heritage.

Ecotourism can also provide resources for environmental conservation and management and an incentive for the conservation and sustainable use of public and private land. To ensure the success of the national policy, the Australian government committed Aus. $10,000,000 over four years for the implementation of the strategy. Following the national lead, each state started to develop a similar regional policy, the latest being the one for New South Wales. Tanzania has a draft national tourism policy document, an integrated master plan, and an infrastructure plan. A key part of this plan is to develop a southern tourism loop to exploit the national parks and wildlife reserves, such as Ruaha National Park and Selous Game Reserve, in the southern part of the country. This new loop will complement the very successful northern loop that contains sites such as Kilimanjaro National Park, the Serengetti National Park, and the Ngorongoro Conservation Area. New Zealand has a very successful nature-based tourism policy that involves high levels of public and private cooperation in the protection of landscapes, the management of protected areas, and the delivery of tourism services. These countries have government policy as the framework for a whole range of public and private activities, and this policy has helped foster a suitable environment for the development of nature-based tourism generally, and park tourism specifically. Government policy plays a very important role in the development of tourism industries that are financially and ecologically sustainable.

Globally, the area of land covered by the world's parks and protected areas increased considerably from 1900 to 1996. By 1996 the world's network of 30,361 parks covers an area of 13,245,527 square kilometres, representing 8.84% of the total land area of the planet. This total land area occurs in 225 countries and dependent territories. The impressive growth of the world's park network is the result of the widespread acceptance of the ecological ethic and aggressive political action. It appears that the tourism activity occurring at these sites created a self-perpetuating phenomenon of visitation, education, and desire for more parks, visitation and education. The global network includes a wide variety of types of protected areas, ranging from nature reserve through to protected landscape, within the International Union for the Conservation of Nature and Natural Resources' (IUCN) six-category system.

Unfortunately, there is no global tabulation of park usage, as there is for park area. Therefore, it is not possible to comprehensively report on the total volume of recreational use in recent years or its change over time. However, individual country reports and the personal communication with many scholars and park managers suggest that park tourism volume has increased considerably over time. The decline was due to a weak economy in the US causing lowered travel to Costa Rica combined with an 800% increase in park entrance fees for foreigners. The visitation recovered and then increased as the economy improved and more suitable pricing policy developed. In 1996 there was an estimated 2,621,777,237 visitor days of recreation activity in the parks and protected areas of Canada and the US. Clearly, the outdoor recreation occurring in the parks and protected areas in Canada and the United States is a very large and impressive activity. With an estimated 2.6 billion days of use per year this activity has major economic, social and environmental impacts. However, until there are international standards for park tourism data collection and management, and global tabulation of these data, this important international activity will suffer from a lack of co-ordination in data reporting and an associated void in public policy profile.

Park Economics

Economics is an important component of societal decision- making, but it is often given low priority in the parks' world. Usually in parks, the very strong emphasis given to ecology is seen by many park proponents as sufficient justification for public policy action. However, nature tourism is increasingly becoming important within sustainable development because of the potential of contributing to local and national economic development while also providing incentive for nature conservation and biodiversity conservation.

Most of the world's protected areas charge low entry and use fees. These fees typically cover only a portion of the cost of protecting the resource and providing the features on which the park visitation depends. This pricing policy developed during a period where resource protection was seen as the overwhelmingly important objective, a public objective that benefits all of society. If a public good benefits all, it can be reasonably argued that it should be paid for by taxes on society. However, this logic falters when applied to outdoor recreation in parks as only those who participate in outdoor recreation are beneficiaries. In a time of widespread government financ ial retrenchment, it is increasingly difficult to justify public expenditure to subsidize the recreation of one segment of the population. Governments around the world are using this logic, in part, for the reduction or freezing of grants for park management.

The reduction of budgets has been documented in Canada and the USA as has the development of new forms of park administration and new pricing policies. The Parks Canada business plan summarizes this concept with the statement that "subsidies will be phased out on services of benefit to individuals, by transferring the operation to the nonprofit voluntary or private sectors, or these services will be stabilized on a full cost recovery basis". There are dramatic differences amongst the world's parks in terms of pricing policy, tourism income, and financial management. A global study of biosphere reserves found that only 32 of 78 responding sites charged visitors admission fees. The fees ranged from less than $5.00 to $110 per person per day, in US funds, with the vast majority at the lower range. There was a statistically significant relationship between total direct income and the numbers of visitors for all biosphere reserves. Higher visitor numbers corresponded to higher budgets. Generally, those parks with high levels of tourism clients gain higher levels of political power. This power is then translated into higher budget allocations. It is important to recognize that substantial management budgets are necessary in areas of high usage to avoid excessive damage to the natural environment of the parks. Parks often supply the most important part of the nature tourism experience, but typically capture little of the economic value of the stream of economic benefits.

The low entry and use fees in parks are the result of many factors, one being the effort of a centralized budget allocation process in many governments. With this form of government financial management, the park management does not keep earned fees within its internal financial structure, and therefore sees little benefit in comprehensive fee collection. This also contributes to a low emphasis on park visitor management. Such issues as retur n rates, length of stay, visit satisfaction and service quality all suffer when the financial return from the visitors is not tied directly to the financial operation of a park. This lack of proper emphasis on visitor management results in a dwarfed park tourism industry, one not fulfilling its potential.

Many governments see nature-based tourism as an important tool for economic development. Unfortunately, most have not invested sufficiently in staff training, infrastructure or park resources that are needed to support nature tourism. This exposes sensitive sites to tourism-caused degradation. Most national tourism agencies do not keep statistics on market sectors, such as those associated with nature-based tourism and park-based tourism. Other management units, such as park agencies seldom fill this information void. As a result, important sectors, such as naturebased tourism, are not clearly documented for the benefit of policy determination. Looking at the Canadian situation can show this situation. Clearly nature-based tourism is one of the key elements of Canadian tourism. The Canadian Tourism Commission provides quarterly Canadian tourism figures to governments, business and the media. These data considerably raise the profile of tourism within the business sector. However, in Canada there is no system for the collection and distribution of information on nature-based or park-based tourism. Neither the volumes of park visitation nor its economic impacts are systematically collected and made available for government and private consumption.

Therefore, the importance of nature tourism in the country is severely underrated due to lack of adequate information. The parks do not compare well to other economic generators, such as auto manufacturing or forestry, where the volumes and economic value of the products are carefully documented and reported within a continuous stream of information. This Canadian situation is common throughout the world. The economic impact of park tourism is not well known, not well documented, and where known, not well communicated. This leads to a severe under-representation of the importance of park tourism within the fiscal sectors of government and business. Globally, the economic studies available on nature tourism. Most of these studies are of individual parks or wildlife reserves. There are few regional or national studies of the economic impact of the tourism associated with parks and reserves. Eagles, McLean & Stabler compiled a national park- use database for Canada and the United States. They found that in 1996, the last year complete data were available, 2,506,451,728 visitor days of recreation occurred in the federal and state parks and protected areas of the USA, and an additional 115,325,509 visitor days of recreation occurred in Canadian federal and provincial protected areas. This massive volume of 2,621,777,237 visitor days, previously undocumented, reveals a high level of tourism use not generally known and appreciated. The economic implications of this usage are normally not calculated and therefore are certainly not well known in the fiscal policy arena of North American society. It is useful to look at some of the park tourism economic impact studies that have been done.

Ontario has a large and well- used provincial park system consisting of 275 parks. In 1992 the total economic output from park users and by government was Can.$831,200,000. A total of 12,172 person-years of employment resulted from parks. This bene fit was calculated from data on the 109 parks that were staffed to manage visitor use in 1992. More economic benefit would be found if the other non-staffed, 166 provincial parks, the six national parks and the hundreds of conservation areas were added to the calculations. Recent research documented the expenditure level of park users to Ontario's Algonquin Provincial Park. This is Ontario's oldest and most visited Provincial Park. This research showed that the park management earned the most income from the groups that spent the least per day, car and interior campers. Conversely, the management earned the least from the people who spent the most, day visitors and lodge visitors. Two important user groups, bus tour visitors and children's camp users were not studied. This analysis shows the need for a complete re-evaluation of the pricing and income policy of this important park.

The provincial economic impact was calculated by the Provincial Economic Impact Model of the Department of Canadian Heritage. The impact generated by Algonquin Park and Friends of Algonquin organizational spending was estimated as Can $4.9 million in labour income, $6.0 million to the Gross Domestic Product and

150 full-time person-years of employment. The provincial economic impact generated by visitor spending was estimated as $8,1 million in labour income, $11.9 million to the Gross Domestic Product and 301 full- time person-years of employment. Therefore, the provincial economic impact generated by park expenditures, Friends expenditures and expenditures by five visitor groups (day users, car campers, interior campers, lodge visitors, and cottage leaseholders) was $13 million in labour, $17.9 in GDP and 451 in person years of employment. This is a conservative estimate. Parks Ontario typically uses the Ministry of Natural Resources Social and Economic Impact model for estimates of economic impact of the provincial parks.

The most recent economic benefits study for a park system undertaken in Canada was done for British Columbia. The BC provincial parks' system is a major source of economic activity in the province. In 1993 the parks generated 5,300 jobs directly and 4,000 jobs indirectly. The 5,300 jobs created by parks are comparable to other industries such as newsprint (4,200), metal mining (3,800) and coal mining (3,000). In 1993 the BC provincial parks' system contributed about Can.$430,000,000 to the provincial gross domestic product. The park visitors reported significant benefits from recreational activities beyond the market transactions. These nonmarket benefits were estimated at Can.$670,000,000 beyond the cost of operating the system by the province. Clearly, British Columbia's provincial parks are a major economic force in the province. If the national parks' contribution was added to the BC provincial parks' contribution, then the benefits would be considerably enhanced.

The Province of Alberta undertook an economic impact calculation of tourism in its provincial parks, following on the lead of British Columbia. The results showed an economic impact that was large and similar to the economic impact of forestry in the province. The report was never officially released. It is speculated that the significance of the information to decision making resulted in a successful lobby effort by the forest industry to make sure that the report was not released, in order to avoid the positive political impact that would occur to parks with the report's dissemination. This is a common problem for park managers, interagency conflict that results in a suppression of data and resources with the goal of now allowing park tourism to gain the full public policy profile that it would otherwise enjoy. This is especially an issue when park management is within a broadly-defined resource management agency. This is least of an issue when parks are a stand alone agency or administration.

Parks Canada conservatively estimates the economic impact of national parks, national historic sites and parks, and national canals to Canada's GDP at Can.$1,250,000,000 per year. Around 30,000 person-years of employment occur due to this spending. Non-resident visitors contribute 25% of the visitor spending, or $275,000,000 annually. These benefits included direct benefits, and consumer surplus. In 1993 the parks had 22,300,000 visitor days of activity. Therefore, each day of recreation produced an economic benefit of Can.$19. In 1992 the total economic output due to Ontario parks was Can.$831,200,000. This amount included direct, indirect, and induced impacts of parks. In 1992 Ontario provincial parks had 7,000,000 visitor days of recreation activity.

Therefore, each day of recreation produced an economic benefit of Can.$119. However, if one takes this range of economic benefits and applies it to the visitation of all Canada's parks, an economic benefit occurs of between Can.$2.2 and $14 billion. However, whichever figure is used, the implications of such a large economic impact on public policy making in Canada are immense. Clearly, a standard and consistent method of calculating economic impact is required, and one has been developed for the application by all provincial and national park agencies in Canada.

In Canada there are several financial structures within the federal and provincial park agencies. Some are government agencies. Others function like crown corporations. The recovery of management costs from tourist charges varies from only 1% in British Columbia, to slightly more than 50% in Saskatchewan This variation is largely due to government policy dictating the financial structure of the agencies, not to the volume of tourism nor to the amount of area being managed. Those with the lowest level of cost recover had very weak tourism expertise within the park agencies, with the result that most tourism income was earned by the private sector. Those with the highest level of cost recovery had revenue retention within the agency, and some form of corporate operations. Clearly, most parks in this sample have the majority of their budget coming from sources other than tourism income. However, globally the trend is for government to demand that parks earn much higher amounts of their budget from tourism sources. Corresponding to this is the development of forms of management, such as parastatals, that allow for park agencies to function with the efficiencies of a private corporation. Parks Canada has designed a management structure that encourages increasingly higher levels of cost recovery from tourists. To provide the management structure necessary to implement the new business approach, Parks Canada obtained government permission (a) to retain and reinvest all revenues, (b) to plan and operate on a multi-year, non- lapsing basis, (c) to increase non-tax revenues from products and services, (d) to borrow against future revenue, (e) to link revenues to costs, and (f) to depreciate assets. The new approach moves this government agency into a management style very similar to that of a corporation, a governmentowned corporation or a parastatal. To implement this plan, new national parks' legislation was passed by the Canadian Parliament in 1998.

Park Finance and Pricing Policy

Typically, in most countries park pricing policy involves a flat fee for entrance, typically for a vehicle, or for facility use, such as for one campsite. In many cases no fees are charged, especially in low- use areas, in popular sites in the low season or in remote areas. The fees are modest and not subject to market forces. Recreation allocation is typically done by the first-come first-serve approach. In some parks fees are also charged by the park agency for specialized recreation services, equipment rental, accommodation, food services and souvenir sales. Typically the income from tourism is well below the park budget, constituting a small percentage of the money used for management. Globally, there is a trend of governments requiring parks to recover higher percentages of their budgets from tourist expenditures. Often the generation of small amounts of revenue provides little incentive for the central government to provide adequate levels of budget for management. The typical budget situation for parks is that of a central government body setting an annual budget, dependent upon the money available for the central treasury as well as various political and lobby group machinations.

In countries without a large tax-based subsidy for park management, tourism is often the largest source of income for park agencies. Throughout Africa, for example, the parks must earn much or most of their operating budgets from tourism. This has led to a level of innovation in pricing policy that is worthy of note. South Africa has a booming tourism industry that has expanded dramatically in the past five years and is predicted to grow substantially in the next five years. Significantly, 60% of the 5.5 million tourists who visited the country in 1997 visited a national park or game reserve. The democratically elected government of South Africa has many social objectives calling for budget allocation. As a result all tax-based grants to the national and provincial park systems are being phased out, leaving the parks with the options of increasing income from tourism or cutting staff and services. The parks are responding with impressive pricing and tourism service innovation.

The South African National Parks (SANP) system is now at 80% budget recovery from tourism. SANP now operates an impressive array of tourism businesses in the national parks. It provides a range of accommodation, ranging from campgrounds through family cabins to hotels. All of the food and souvenir stores are agency operated. Many of the tours are park operated. Therefore, income is earned from entrance fees, lodging, food provision, product sales and tours. In the future, licensing of intellectual property, such as logos and park names, is a possibility. Special promotional co-operation with associated industries, such as 4 by 4 vehicle companies, holds promise. This diverse set of income generators must be further utilized if the SANP is to gain sufficient income to reach the public policy goal of financial self- sufficiency.

Differential fees are becoming more common. Foreigners pay more, and sometimes much more, than nationals do. At high demand times prices are sometimes higher. Prices are becoming associated with service level, higher prices corresponding to more services. Those agencies that have parastatal status and have private sector involvement have a much higher diversity of pricing and servicing standards. South Africa is a good example of the development of a wide range of standards and pricing for accommodation in and near the parks. The parks typically provide three levels of basic accommodation services: personal tent camping, RV camping, and semi-permanent tent rentals, the latter of which typically are wood-floored, canvas tents. The parks sometimes also have three different levels of roofed accommodation, ranging from rustic cabins through cottages to hotels.

Many parks provide several levels of food provision, from restaurants, through fast food outlets to grocery stores. Merchandise sales are common, typically for typical outdoor gear and souvenirs. In South Africa the private sector is heavily involved in the upper range market, providing two or three levels of highly priced accommodations and associated ecotourism services at private game reserves. The private reserves are often located adjacent to the parks, to take advantage of the wildlife and ecosystems of the parks as well as the already identified ecotourism profile of the location. The names and images of national parks are some of the most well-known and powerful in the world. Private corporations will often pay high sums for the use of these names and images. Cross marketing occurs when one product or organization advertises in concert with another. An example could be a park agency using one type of recreational vehicle, thereby advertising to all the visitors its special qualities in the park environment. In concert, the vehicle manufacturer would publicize the park as the point is made about the special features of a vehicle. Australia is a typical example with most park agencies in the country relying on only a few of these sources of income, typically entrance fees, some recreation service fees and accommodation fees, usually for camping. Australia has a long tradition of free public access to na tural and cultural heritage assets, so much so that when the Great Barrier Reef National Marine Park proposed an increase from $1 to $6 for park visitors using commercial tourist operators a Senate parliamentary committee inquiry was launched.

There are implications for management of higher levels of income based on tourism. Overall, park visitors will face higher fees and more increased opportunity where fees are charged. The biggest changes take place within the park agency. A business approach to management is necessary. This includes the ability to retain and utilize most if not all income. Given the need for income, the park visitors become more important. Their opinions on programs, their length of stay, their return rates, their facility and program needs and their overall satisfaction become important management variables. The managers become more aware of the need for marketing, that is the creation of a product that fits the market needs. Once the income becomes substantial park management has a higher level of independence from government grants, and from government in general. Experience reveals many resistance factors from the move from a park agency dependent upon government grants, to an agency dependent upon tourism income. Nature is perceived as being universally-owned and requiring no human management. This concept of nature as a free good creates expectations that national parks and other forms of protected areas should provide free access. Over history this concept was reinforced with pricing for access well below the production cost. In the USA national park use fees were prohibited by law for many years.

The private sector in tourism usually objects to any fees, and especially to any increase in fees. In addition, it is obvious to many business people in tourism that substantial income can be earned by providing services to park visitors. These people therefore act like vultures, swooping into the political arena to seize the most important assets, such as accommodation and food provision. This denies the park management from important income sources. Park agencies are typically not equipped to undertake business management. Their marketing, pricing policy, economics and financial expertise are usually deficient. This and other factors lead many park agency staff to vigorously object to a park agency operating as a business. It is common for important sectors of the public, such as environmental groups, to object to the business operation. This is often due to fears of over commercialisation. It can also be due to resistance to paying increased fees.

Tourism Planning

All national parks and protected areas have some level of visitor use. This can vary from just a few to millions of visitors per year. Much of the visitor management is reactive, rather than proactive. The parks receive whatever visitor use that occurs, and then try to develop mechanisms to define and manage appropriate activities and levels of use. Often visitor management only takes place when some level of a problem is perceived. The parks usually provide "take it or leave it" levels of tourism service. In other words, a type of recreation program or facility and a level of service is provided, with the visitor free to accept this, or to not participate. Visitors are expected to make their opinions about activities and services known through management reviews or through complaints, or not at all. It is very rare for park agencies to consis tently and professionally evaluate and monitor the wants and levels of satisfaction of their visitors. It is even rarer for evaluation to be done on potential visitors or past visitors who did not return. The majority of park agencies are weak in tourism competencies. Those that do occur are usually the result of resource managers learning on the job about visitors and tourism management. Very few agencies, and almost no parks, have professional expertise in leisure pricing policy, in tourism economics, in marketing, in tourism management, in social statistics, in service quality or in leisure studies. However, this situation is changing rapidly in several countries.

The low level of tourism competency occurs in park agencies where the emphasis is on resource protection and the budget comes entirely from a central government pot. However, whenever a park agency starts to move to a tourism-based budget where income from visitor services provides the income, there is a much higher emphasis given to tourism management. Often the private sector operators in and near the parks have much higher levels of tourism market expertise than do the parks. In many parts of the world the private sector is the force behind the tourism in parks. It is the private sector that attracts the visitors, services their basic needs, and provides all of the tourism services.

Park Tourism Market

Is there a market for increased levels of nature-based tourism? The largest market study ever undertaken was done for British Columbia and Alberta in Canada in 1995. The term ecotourism was used and was defined very broadly as "nature, adventure and cultural experiences in the countryside". The study found a very large ecotourism market in Canada and the United States. In the seven metropolitan areas studied, Seattle, San Francisco, Los Angeles, Dallas, Chicago, Toronto, and Winnipeg a market of 13.2 million potential ecotravellers was found. This was much larger than anticipated, and showed that a large market is now present in North America alone. The study found that the natural setting is the most critical factor in the determination of a quality product. The tourists showed increasing desire to find experiences in environments that were ecologically well managed. Recreational activities were important and multiple activities were desired. Midrange accommodation was desired, and the experienced ecotourist placed much higher emphasis on the outdoor experience than on the accommodation. Competent guides and quality interpretive programs enhanced the quality of the travel product experience. The preferred trip was long, at seven days or more. Parks and the activities in the parks were found to be very important components of the ecotravel experience. Clearly, there is a large and growing ecotourism market in North America.

Travel trends throughout the world point to growing markets, especially in North America, Europe and Asia. Given the large potential market size, the key issue becomes one of providing travel products that fit the market and ensuring that these products have positive economic and environmental benefits.

Decisions should be based upon data. The better the data, the better the chance of good decisions. A fundamental figure for decision making is that of product volume. No private company can survive without thorough, accurate and up-to-date data on the numbers and timing of the production and subsequent sale of the ir products. However, some parks pay low levels of attention to documenting their level of recreation use. In recent years during budget cutting some managers cut gate staff and visitor management personnel, people doing functions seen as less important. Imagine a store firing all its cashiers and its product service personnel! Many parks are poorly designed for documentation of visitation levels. Parks are often large with many entry points, making it difficult to tabulate all entrances. Some park clients sneak in, to avoid fees. Many parks do not have staff covering all entrances at all times of the day and all months of the year. Shoulder season visitation is usually poorly documented. Within one agency there may be different data collection procedures in different parks. And in large parks there may be different data collection procedures at different entrances. However, the recent move in Canada and the USA towards parks retaining fee income is reversing this trend and placing much higher emphasis on catching as many of the clients as possible.

One major reason for the increase is the fees charged were used to provide higher levels of service, especially for camping. Every park system has its own, unique system of counting and recording its visitors. Some count all who enter, including recreationists, service vehicles, and vehicles just passing through. Some count only those who stay during the night, ignoring day visitors. Some count only those who pay. Some record the numbers of entrants, some the numbers of visitor hours, and others the numbers of visitor days. There is a need to standardize, in parks, in countries, and globally, the definition, the collection procedures, and the reporting of park tourism statistics. When this is done, the park movement will have new and powerful data for influencing public policy discussions. Recently the World Commission on Protected Areas released the first-ever guidelines for the measurement of public use of parks and protected areas. This manual provides standardized terminology for park tourism, outlines a five- level system of sophistication for measurement, provides guidance on measurement techniques and technologies, and provides examples of the use of tourism data in park management. The guidelines are intended to assist in the standardization of park tourism measurement. In 2001 a global tabulation of park tourism use levels will be undertaken as part of the preparation of the next edition of the United Nations list of national parks and protected areas. The goal is to have the global park- use data available for the next World Parks Congress that is to be held in South Africa in September 2003.

Tourism Management Structures

Typically parks are managed by government agencies. In this situation most staff are government employees with a hierarchical form of decision- making. Budgets are provided each year from a central government allocation, with park income being returned to a central government pot. Often visitor services, such as accommodation, tours and consumer products, are provided by concessionaires who are licensed by the agency for a period of time. This model is widespread and reasonably effective when central government provides sufficient budget. However, it is very ineffective in several respects. The budgets are not closely tied to tourism levels, so park management is severely limited in its ability to respond to increases or other changes in visitation levels. Also the park staff recognize that the key people to please are those who provide the budget, such as upper level bureaucrats and politicians. As a result the level of understanding and commitment to park visitors is often very low with this model of management. This model can be problematic when the size and power of the private sector tourism overwhelms a politically weak government agency. In this situation the selfish individual interests of the tourism operators can lead to tourism overuse. Very severe environmental degradation often occurs with this model, due to the lack of budget for the agency to handle tourism pressures. Much experimentation with park management structures is under way. Three new models that are having success are worthy of discussion: the parastatal agency, the non-profit corporation, and the private, for-profit corporation.

Many government agencies are shifting to a parastatal form of operation, as discussed earlier for

Canada. A parastatal is a corporate body within government. The parastatal makes its own policy, maintains internal financial operations, and has control over internal reporting and decision structures. Often a government-appointed Board of Directors functions as the overall policy and approving body, sometimes with veto powers held by a Minister. This approach is in place in Kenya, in Tanzania, in South Africa and in Ontario, Canada, to name four examples. Advantages over the government model are numerous. This structure is much more financially efficient. The agency can quickly establish pricing and tourism policies that enable it to more effectively tap tourism financial flows. The ability to internally handle budgets means a better understanding of the connection between service and income, between outflow and inflow of money. This structure usually leads to much higher levels of emphasis on park visitors, their needs and their satisfaction. This approach often has a much flatter structure, with the multiple layers of the government agency replaced by only a couple of administrative layers.

The biggest disadvantage of a parastatal, seen by some, is the loss of central control by government. Those countries with parastatal forms of park agency management are those that are most likely to earn the majority or their entire operational budget from tourism. Examples include Tanzania National Parks (TANAPA) in Tanzania, Kenya Wildlife Service (KWS) in Kenya, and SANP in South Africa. However, it is important to note that in all three of these African countries various forms of foreign aid are very important for capital development in the parks. Some countries utilize non-profit corporations to provide some of the tourism services. These can take the form of membership groups that provide specialized services, such as guiding, information dispersal, and recreation management. Such groups have the advantages of a parastatal plus the additional ability to mobilize large numbers of volunteers and solicit donations. However, this approach is rarely used for entire parks, probably due to the narrow focus of such groups and their lack of ability to handle the entire range of concerns required in park management.

Often for-profit private corporations provide some tourism products and services to visitors in parks. This is frequently done on a licensed concessionaire basis, where the company has a monopoly, or on a free market basis where many companies compete for the tourist market. Occasionally experimentation is occurring where park development or park management is being turned over totally to private companies. One such case is now taking place in Lesotho. The Lesotho Highlands Development Authority is constructing a series of massive dams in the Lesotho highlands, for the purpose of earning income from the export of water to the large urban areas of nearby South Africa. As a remediation effort the Authority has hired a consulting firm to select, plan, design and construct a system of protected areas within the development area. Four parks are under development, with two, the Bokong Nature Reserve and Tse'hylane National Park, at the stage of tourism facility development. At the end of the contract period the private firm will turn over the operational parks to the fledgling national parks' agency of the country.

Park Tourism Opportunities

Within most park agencies the park management authorities have some level of familiarity with park visitation. Most are capable of handling some international tourism. If the parks work within a competent, co-ordinated system, and have sufficient finances to operate the parks that exist, it is possible to develop a co-ordinated tourism management system.

For the parks to become international destinations, the country and the parks must have a global image of being a premier destination for outdoor recreation and nature tourism. Potential tourists must see some international profile. Location is important, but poor location can be overcome due to inexpensive air travel.

Significant natural resources, a high market profile, and a quality service industry are three prerequisites for effective utilization of the international market. The international airports, road, and water transportation system must be capable of handling significant levels of tourism traffic. Information systems need to be able to handle the whole range of needs that occur in tourism. People need lots of information. Those sites that have better information technologies are much more effective in attracting international tourism.

Unfortunately, most park agencies do not control the flow of the majority of information that is provided to park visitors. Guide books, feature films, conservation groups, scientific publications, and tour companies usually provide more information than do the parks. This can be an advantage if the information is accurate and appropriate, but it can be very problematic if the park is not prepared or capable of handling the resultant tourism traffic. It can also be a problem if the information is wrong, or purposely misleading.

Park Tourism Challenges

Most parks are not now equipped to handle international tourism. Typically these parks lack tourism management capability, sufficient staff, and infrastructure. Examples to illustrate this lack of expertise are easy to find. Many parks do not have the language ability to handle tourism from foreign countries. Often very little is done to encourage and assist visitation by people from foreign countries. Most parks have insufficient numbers of people with expertise in tour ism, marketing, service quality evaluation, and international ecotourism. The level of expertise in these areas must be considerably upgraded if the agencies want to develop a vibrant, international tourism industry, one that can compete globally. Expertise in service quality management is particularly needed.

The North American service industries are the global leaders in the development and application of service quality management principles. As a result, the North American consumer expects high levels of quality from service providers. Government agencies lag far behind the private sector in applying service quality management principles, and this lack is obvious to their clients. Several countries, most specifically the USA, Australia, and the United Kingdom, have aggressive tourism research, education, and development programs aimed at nature-based tourism.

Many parks are generally unknown outside the local area, and have weak mechanisms to provide a higher level of profile. Many parks have natural resources of limited international appeal. Therefore, it is reasonable to suggest that only some parks can play an international role. Within an overall park system tourism strategy, only those with appropriate natural and managerial resources should be chosen for international visitation.

Only a few parks have an existing international reputation sufficient to attract people to the sites as primary travel destinations. Those that have the names "national park" and "World Heritage Site" have significant brand identity. The plethora of park names, such as "provincial park" and "conservation area," leads to confusion by many potential visitors. These names are often poorly known outside the local area. These phrases may also connote low levels of resource significance and tourism infrastructure.

Parks are very important components of the nature-based tourism industry. They occupy some of the most interesting landscapes. They also have information and infrastructure that attract tourists. And they can be used within a system of linked travel routes for long-distance travel. However, the parks are seldom managed within a system of linked travel routes.

Many park administrations show weak understanding of the global ecotourism market. There does not appear to be a policy envelope, an administrative structure, or a staffing complement that recognizes an international role. The big exception to this situation is in Australia, with both national and state-level ecotourism strategies that explicitly deal with the parks as international destinations. The ecotourism policy and plan for the State of Queensland in Australia is one of the most mature policy documents available. An obvious example of the lack of understanding of international tourism is the inadequacy of programs and facilities aimed in this direction. International visitation is not directed through a well-designed system of information for international visitors.

Multilingual publications are almost non-existent. Staff language ability is generally in the local language, often in English, and almost never in other important languages such as German, Spanish, or Japanese. Prebooking by international visitors is very difficult or non-existent. There is no way for international tourists to work through their travel agents to facilitate visitation to most parks. Often visitors are expected to bring all the necessary equipment for camping or outdoor recreation, a very difficult and expensive task for trips that involve air travel. Rental or sale of equipment sometimes occurs in the parks, but its availability is spotty, and when available, is difficult to access for international visitors.

There is seldom easy access to guides, specialized information, or ethnic food for international travellers. Co-operation with airlines, tour agencies, recreation vehicle rental companies, or hotel chains is rare. Parks do little to encourage, or even facilitate, the visitation by people from the country's major foreign tourism markets. However, if these challenges were tackled effectively by the parks, the numbers of international visitors could increase dramatically.

Often the parks' infrastructure is designed for the knowledgeable and experienced local person. It is difficult for foreigners to visit parks. It is very difficult for them to gain the knowledge of a park, to obtain access, to get all the necessary equipment, to learn how to use the equipment, to gain suitable transport and then to visit most parks. In North America camping is the dominant form of camping in parks. The complexity of camping redirects many visitors into other forms of accommodation. However, there is very limited roofed accommodation in the parks to handle the international ecotourism market. There are often suitable accommodations outside the parks, but these are typically small scale and difficult to access by people in remote locales of the world. Park tourism is a global phenomenon and has a global market. Those agencies and those parks that develop suitable expertise and facilities are out-competing others.

The phenomenal success of national parks and game reserves in South Africa in the last half decade shows how a sophisticated tourism approach can successfully out-compete many other similar destinations in Africa that have equally good natural resources, but less effective tourism operations. Some of the deficiencies outlined are due to low levels of finance. At present, the typical government agency structure results in insufficient finance to hire trained staff, to develop the research base, to develop the product line, to advertise the product, and to handle the visitors when they arrive. The parastatal agency structures developing in many countries help selffinance this endeavour when they become operational, but there are often insufficient start-up funds. It is important for governments to recognize that one must spend money to make money. Allocations from governments are necessary for the development of nature-based tourism. These allocations must be made within the context of a carefully constructed national, provincial, and agency policy environment. This aid is often occurring in developing countries through various forms of foreign aid. The Global Environment Facility provides grants and soft loans for biodiversity conservation in parks and protected areas, with the long-term operational funds to come from tourism. The challenges are partially due to a nature-tourism policy void in many countries.

There is an urgent need for co-ordinated national/provincial/regional nature-based tourism strategies in most countries. These strategies would identify key policy priorities, consider which sites have potential for international ecotourism, develop recommendations for market development, provide backing to financial development, and schedule a multi-year development plan. The Australian national and state nature-tourism policies are the best in the world at the current time.

If park tourism is to be given the level of public policy recognition that it deserves, a more consistent and thorough procedure for the collection of visitation and economic data is required. After his study of economic evaluation of recreation and tourism in New South Wales he called for "a more consistent approach to data collection."

The World Commission on Protected Areas is attempting to standardize the collection and use of park tourism data. Guidelines for the measurement of economic impact of parks are under development. The goal of this effort is to standardize methods of measurement and to encourage the widespread collection and dissemination of the output.

Guidelines for the collection and use of visitor-use data are published by the World Commission on Protected Areas. The goals of these two efforts are to standardize the approaches used for economic impact measurement, as well as the terminology, the measurement methods, and the reporting of park visitation. These guidelines should be of assistance to all parks agencies. The development of management effectiveness guidelines and procedures can assist policy makers, senior management, and the public in understanding the capability of park managers and their institutions.

Many parks are starting to move towards agency management structures that function like corporations within government. This involves a) agency retention of fee and license revenue, b) retention of budget surpluses at the end of the fiscal year, c) pricing policies that better reflect the cost of production, and d) more flexible arrangements with corporate and nonprofit entities outside government. It is probable that higher use fees will be charged. Over time a much higher proportion of revenue will come from merchandise and food sales than now occurs. Innovative funding mechanisms, such as licensing of park names or cooperative public-private ventures in special purpose merchandise, are under way.

Park agencies must develop tourism management competencies within their own organization. It is critical that the park visitors' needs and wants be understood. Most park agencies now function on a take- it or leave- it philosophy towards their visitors. Certain types of facilities and services are provided, and the park client is not eve n asked if this facility or service is desirable or serving their needs. A class example to illustrate this point is the lack of service quality management in most park agencies. Few agencies have specific service quality goals, with Parks Canada being a notable exception. The private sector in leisure services is rapidly moving towards service quality goal management. All park agencies require specialists in leisure pricing policy. Pricing policy is a major field in business management, and a critical component of the operation of most corporations. Leisure marketing is the specialised field concerned with developing a solid understanding of the client, the product and developing means to match the two. The park agencies with parastatal forms of management are now staffing with specialized expertise in leisure marketing.

Tourism management is a large and specialized field that is a broad and complex as resource management. All park agencies should develop staff expertise in this area. It may be too obvious a point to make, but it is important to note that people trained in biology. Therefore, it is important for park agencies to retrain their existing staff, or hire such expertise. The negative impact of tourism on park resources is less influenced by absolute numbers of visitors, and more influenced by weak tourism policy, management and staffing. Very low levels of finance often cause this. It has been shown many times in many parks that with sufficient expertise and finance, park tourism can be very competently managed, with low levels of negative environmental impact and high levels of positive economic impact.

The key issue is developing a management framework that emphasizes staff expertise in tourism and financial competence. Tourism, within most park agencies, can provide significant levels of income if it's allowed to by the overall government legislative and policy framework. The next 20 years will see a major shift in park management towards much more sophisticated tourism management. Such a shift will help considerably in developing a financial system that allows for competent and successful park management.

5

Tourism Scenario: India

The travel and tourism sector creates more jobs per million rupees of investment than any other sector of the economy and is capable of providing employment to a wide spectrum of job seekers from the unskilled to the specialised, even in the remote parts of the country.

The Tenth Plan approach towards tourism signifies a distinct shift from the approach adopted in earlier Plans. Apart from acknowledging the well-accepted advantages of developing tourism for the promotion of national integration, international understanding and earning foreign exchange, the Tenth Plan recognises the vast employment generating potential of tourism and the role it can play in furthering the socio-economic objectives of the Plan.

In order to create a supportive environ-ment for the promotion of tourism, the New Tourism Policy, 2002, that is to be implemented during the Tenth Plan, will generate awareness about the benefits of tourism for the host population. It will mobilise state governments to use tourism as a means for achieving their socio-economic objectives, encourage the private sector to enhance investment in tourism and provide legislative and regulatory support for sustainable tourism and to protect the interests of the industry and the consumer.

The policy envisages involving the rural sector in the promotion of rural, heritage, adventure and eco-tourism and will promote the development of competitive high quality products and destina-tions. Most importantly, it will remove the barriers to growth and resolve contradictions in policy to achieve inter-sectoral convergence of activities that help the growth of tourism.

The initiatives taken by the state so far have not yielded the desired result and India's tourism performance has failed to match its potential even as countries not blessed with its natural and cultural endowments have taken the lead in reaping the benefits of tourism development for their people. The reasons for this poor performance need to be speedily addressed to enable tourism to make an appropriate contribution to national development.

As observed in the Planning Commission Report of the National Committee on Tourism (1988), the public sector made a significant contribution to the growth of tourism in the initial stages of planned development by providing a reasonable infrastructure base. During the Ninth Plan it was recognised that a reappraisal of the role of the State in tourism development and the extent of its participation was needed as it is neither necessary nor feasible for the State to make large investments in areas that are best left to the initiative of the private sector.

The state can contribute through infrastructure development, the planning of broad development strategies, the provision of fiscal and monetary incentives to catalyse private sector investment and devise an effective regulatory and supervisory mechanism to protect the interests of the industry and the consumer. The acceptance of this view also led to the commencement of the process of disinvestment in 18 hotels of the India Tourism Development Corporation (ITDC) hotels.

The ITDC will have to redefine its role in the Tenth Plan. The State can also play an effective role in ensuring that tourism development does not harm the environment. The interaction between tourism and environmental pollution requires sensitive handling. There is comp-lementarity, not conflict, between the high quality environmental requirements of tourism and the imperatives of maintaining the ecological balance.

Global Status and Trends

Although global recession and the September 11, 2001, events are estimated to have resulted in a temporary decline in travel and tourism demand in 2001-02, international and domestic tourism is expected to boom over the next two decades.

The World Travel and Tourism Council (WTTC) estimates a 4.5 per cent per annum increase in the total amount of travel and tourism economic activity between 2002 and 2012. This is largely attributed to a rise in global wealth, liberali-sation of international airspace, cheaper flights and the use of the Internet as a travel tool.

The earnings from tourism have made it one of the world's largest industries and the fastest growing sectors of global trade accounting for 10.7 per cent of global gross domestic product (GDP), 12.8 per cent of global exports, 8.2 per cent of global employment (or one in every 12.2 jobs), and 9.4 per cent of global capital investment.

Tourism in the least developed countries growing faster than the world average, holding the promise of prosperity for many. International tourist arrivals worldwide reached 698 million in 2000, generating $ 595 billion revenues.

International tourism flows are expected to reach 1.5 billion by 2020 and revenue estimated to cross 2000 billion. Today, only 3.5 per cent of the world population travels internationally but the number of Asian, particularly Chinese, tourists is predicted to grow enormously as the region becomes more integrated with the global economy.

The scale of world domestic tourism, on the other hand, exceeds world international tourism by a ratio of 10:1. In India, for every interna-tional tourist, there are 80 domestic tourists. Domestic tourism can form the basis of a viable and sustainable tourism industry in India.

Global Market Trends

Consumer trends in tourism are gradually changing and require an appropriate response in terms of both policy formulation and investment.

Current market trends indicate that:

— Long haul travel will grow faster than intra-regional travel. A growth of 24 per cent is expected by 2020.

— People with less time for leisure are likely to take more frequent but shorter trips nearer home, opening up opportunities for 'neighbouring country' tourism.

— The experienced traveller wants authentic, off-the-beaten-track vacations in remote and less well-known places as against luxurious five-star vacations, leading to an interest in rural and ethnic tourism.

— The increase in the number of people with lots of money but little leisure time has resulted in a growing emphasis on rest and relaxation, and 'wellness' and 'health' holidays.

— The elderly population in key tourism-generating markets has shown preference for cultural tourism against sun-and-sand vacations.

— There is notable and increasing interest in spiritualism.

— The demand for eco-tourism and nature-based holidays is expected to double and even triple in the next 20 years.

— Sports and adventure holidays continue to be popular with the young.

The interest in cultural tourism, spiritua-lism, 'wellness' holidays, eco-tourism and rural tourism would tend to favour India, provided the country can avail of the opportunities offered maximise its natural advantages in these areas.

The development of new tourism products and destinations during the Tenth Plan must be based on market research and demand, keeping the source markets and the age groups of the tourists in mind. At the same time, the Government must develop new source markets nearer home and make India a safer destination for women tourists and family holidays.

India's Place In World Tourism

The World Tourism Organisation forecast indicates an increasing tourism preference towards East Asia, the Pacific, West Asia and South Asia, although Europe and America still remain the world's foremost tourism destinations commanding 77 per cent of the global market. East Asia/Pacific achie-ved the highest rate of growth of 14.5 per cent in tourism and travel in 2000 followed by West Asia and South Asia.

With this gradual shift in focus, the outlook for the growth of tourism in the region is promising. In Asia, China has emerged as a leading tourist destination and is poised to become the world's top tourist destination by 2020.

The WTTC has identified India as one of the world's foremost tourist growth centres in the coming decade. After Turkey, India is expected to achieve the fastest rate of growth of the total amount of economic activity likely to be generated by travel and tourism, at 9.7 per cent over the next 10 years. Also, the largest employment creation after China is expected to take place in India over the same period.

The growth in 'visitor exports' or spending by international tourists, is likely to be the fastest in India at 14.3 per cent per annum over the next decade. On the whole, the WTTC forecast for India is promising, subject to key policy issues that affect the growth of the sector being addressed.

If India is to realise its enormous potential in tourism it must provide exclusive world-class tourism products and destinations to compete successfully for a larger share of the Asian tourism market. Today, outbound tourism from India far exceeds visitor traffic to the country partly because there is a lack of world-class destinations within the country and partly because the domestic tourism policy has been largely directed towards those in the lower end of the spending spectrum.

The high spender from India prefers to visit neighbouring countries as he gets better value for money. The scope and reach of domestic tourism will have to be broadened in the Tenth Plan through the development of competitive destinations that match international standards in terms of price and quality and also satisfy the international traveller.

India's international arrival figures have not been able to keep pace with neighbouring countries and have been exceeded by Thailand, Malaysia, Indonesia, Dubai and the Maldives. Since 1995, India's share of the world market has remained virtually stagnant at 0.38 per cent, while domestic tourism has grown at a phenomenal rate and India now accounts for 4.6 per cent share of domestic tourism worldwide.

In terms of tourism receipts, India has shown relative buoyancy because of the interest shown by visitors in traditional handicraft items and particularly in diamonds. The Tenth Plan visualises a mutually supportive role for tourism and handicrafts by encouraging haats and shilpgrams and recognising shopping as an integral part of the tourism experience to promote the 'Made in India' brand.

India's Tourist Profile

India receives the largest number of overseas tourists from the United Kingdom, which is its largest source market, followed by the United States, Sri Lanka, France, Germany, Canada, Japan, Australia and Singapore. Of the tourists coming to India, 27.5 per cent are in the age group of 35-44 years, 23.4 per cent in the age group of 25-35 years and 20.8 per cent in the age group of 45-54 years. Women constitute only 30.5 per cent of India's total international arrivals. Repeat visitors account for 44.9 per cent of the overseas visitors.

A substantial number of these may be non-resident Indians, as hotel reservations do not correspond to the number of international arrivals in the country. The average length of stay of foreign tourists in the country in 1998 was 31.2 days. Domestic tourism, on the other hand, is largely pilgrimage-oriented and requires improvement in travel facilities and pilgrim destinations.

Tenth Plan Objective

Tourism in India has tended to be regarded as an elitist activity conducted primarily for the purpose of earning foreign exchange. Its vast potential as an engine of growth and employment generater has remained largely untapped.

Although, with 25 million jobs, India ranks second in terms of number of persons employed in travel and tourism, yet the contribution of the sector as percentage share of all employment is amongst the lowest in the world.

The Tenth Plan objective is to integrate tourism with the socio-economic objectives of the Plan by creating 3.6 million jobs a year through the promotion of domestic and international tourism and to enhance India's share of international arrivals from 0.38 per cent to at least 0.62 per cent by 2007.

Role of the Department of Tourism

Being the nodal agency for the develop-ment of tourism in the country, the department of tourism needs to make greater efforts to co-ordinate and integrate the policies of central ministries that have an impact on the development of tourism and to mobilise state governments and the private sector to develop unique and competitive tourism products and destinations.

Crucial decisions affecting tourism are taken by other ministries viz. the Ministries of Finance, Home, Civil Aviation, Surface Transport, Environment and Forests, Urban Development, Rural Development, Ocean Develop-ment etc.

The Department of Tourism has tended to concentrate largely on its role as the promoter of international tourism and generator of foreign exchange earnings while paying relatively less attention to inter-sectoral policy co-ordination and the all-important development of tourism infrastructure and product quality. In the Tenth Plan, the Department will redefine and expand its role and work towards inter-sectoral convergence and policy integration to remove the barriers to the growth of tourism.

Barriers To Growth

There are several factors that are respon-sible for the inadequate growth of the tourism sector in India. These are: barriers related to approach, barriers that discourage private investment, factors that affect competitiveness and factors that affect the long-term sustainability of tourism.

The effective and early removal of these barriers during the Tenth Plan is an essential determinant for the success of the New Tourism Policy. The need for a national consensus on the role and level of tourism development in the country has been voiced repeatedly but a concerted effort to achieve a consensus has not been made.

Tourism should not be limited by state or regional boundaries if distortions in policies are to be avoided. It is important that a consensus among all states is evolved through the National Development Council (NDC) and the barriers to the growth of tourism removed.

Approach-related barriers:

— Absence of consensus on role of tourism

— Lack of priority to tourism on account of unappreciated potential

— Relatively low levels of investment.

— Lack of interest on the part of the state governments – the primary players.

— An unprofessional ad hoc approach.

Tourism has been denied the priority it deserves over successive Plan periods because its potential as an engine of economic growth has not been appreciated. This is visible in the low allocation of resources. Allocation to tourism has averaged 0.16 per cent of the total Plan outlay from the Third Plan to the Ninth Plan. In the Tenth Plan, it is likely to receive an allocation of 0.72 per cent. According to the WTTC, India is one of the lowest spenders on tourism - 153rd out of 160 countries - while its neighbouring competitors and China invest far more:

Malaysia (5.1 per cent), Nepal (5 per cent), Indonesia (8.4 per cent), Maldives (15.7 per cent), China (3.8 per cent). The growing domestic and international demand, which is set to boom, reinforces the need for higher investment. Failure to measure up to additional investment demand for domestic tourism is likely to lead to the over-exploitation of existing facilities, discouraging foreign visitors while leading to an increase in the outflow of high-spending domestic tourists from the country.

Most State Governments give scant importance to tourism even though they virtually control the tourism product located within their boundaries. They are responsible, inter alia, for local infrastructure, transport systems, sanitation and hygiene, leisure and recreation, law and order, the upkeep of local monuments and the general well-being of the tourist. Their support and participation is essential for tourism to succeed and spread its benefits among the host population. Their lack of interest has resulted in an unprofessional ad hoc approach that acts as a deterrent to the growth of tourism. The approach of the state governments needs to be focused, highly professional and result-oriented if India is to avail of the opportunity that the currently favourable market trends have to offer.

Apart from the State Governments, the private sector plays a vital role in the growth and development of tourism. Although the Central Government and certain state governments have, from time to time, announced incentives to involve the private sector in tourism development, the results achieved have fallen short of expectations.

To provide a conducive environment for private sector investment, it is important to realise that the travel and tourism sector is adversely affected by the lack of synergy in inter-sectoral policies. The growth of the sector requires well-integrated and co-ordinated policies and stability in approach.

Contradictions and arbitrary changes in policy send confused signals to the investor. Unless infirmities in policy are expeditiously removed well before the end of the Tenth Plan period, the New Tourism Policy is unlikely to succeed.

Barriers that discourage private investment:

— Absence of legislative support

— Lack of policy integration and co-ordination

— Lack of long-term investor-friendly policies.

— Heavy and multiple taxes, restrictive aviation and land policies.

Being a long haul destination, India is more conveniently accessible by air and cannot be easily reached by rail or road. A restrictive air transport policy has a very deleterious effect on tourist traffic. There are insufficient connections to most tourism destinations. The situation could be eased if the large number of regional airports could open up as international airports. The existing international and national airports also require improvement. The price of aviation turbine fuel needs to be lowered to make air transport compe-titive and affordable.

Today, it is cheaper to travel by air to neighbouring countries from India than to travel to certain parts of India itself. A more liberal aviation bilaterals regime and a new aviation policy to benefit the economy of the country as a whole rather than the national carriers alone would greatly aid the development of tourism.

Central and state governments need to evolve a taxation regime, which is revenue generating without being burden-some. Accommodation and transport taxes tend to be very heavy in certain states while the excise policy in others is extremely harsh. The land policy in some states makes the setting up of a hotel formidable exercise and as many as 48 clearances are required for the construction and running of hotel. Such policies deter private sector investment.

The importance of protecting private investment in tourism must also be appreciated and activities such as mining, unauthorised construction, encroach-ments and haphazard development around tourist resorts must be prevented through appropriate legislation and public support.

Factors that affect competitiveness:

— Lack of concern for competitiveness

— Complex visa procedures

— Inadequate facilitation services

— Lack of quality infrastructure

— Lack of emphasis on product quality

— Lack of training at the 'cutting edge'

— Lack of hygiene

— Low utilisation of modern marketing and publicity tools.

As tourism is a highly competitive industry; the traveller has a wide range of choices and looks for good value for money. The lack of quality infra-structure, uncompetitive rates, indifferent or poor product quality, difficulty in getting access to information on travel and tourist destinations, untrained service providers, and above all, the lack of hygiene, have an enormously negative effect on the competitiveness of the tourism product.

A world class destination requires professional planning to prevent haphazard, uncontrolled growth, spatial and land use planning, strict architectural controls, sewerage infrastructure and water treatment plants. It requires improvement of entry points and appropriate facilitation services.

The lack of a visa-on-arrival regime on account of security considera-tions places India at a disadvantage vis-à-vis its competitors. It is necessary that India strikes a balance between security considerations and the need for tourism development and reviews its visa policy to permit tourists from its major source markets to obtain visas on arrival. Equally important is the behaviour of the host population.

Training programmes are required not only for hotel mana-gers but also for tourist guides, taxi-drivers, staff at eating places, porters etc., as the manner in which they conduct themselves affects the tourist's experience of the country. Important do's and dont's in terms of a code of ethics need to be inculcated among the service providers. During the Tenth Plan, the Department of Tourism will organise capacity-building programmes for service providers through mobile training units.

A major impediment to the growth of tourism in India has been the lack of awareness about the benefits that it can bestow upon the host population. Unless the host population, both in rural and urban areas, is supportive of tourism, cannot become a vibrant economic force.

The rural sector, in particular, has been largely ignored tourism development and has consequently been deprived of the benefits of employment and income generation accruing from tourism. The Tenth Plan seek to rectify this, particularly in view of the world-wide interest in rural tourism.

While an awareness campaign that elicits local support for travel and tourism is essential for the long-term growth of the sector, it is also important to create awareness about the environmental impact of tourism by generating respect for the carrying capacities of tourist destinations. This is imperative excessive exposure of ecologically fragile areas human interference can lead to irreparable environmental degradation.

As the demand for eco-tourism is expected to grow enormously in the next decade, it is important to have regulations in place prevent such damage. The local population must convinced of the need to support such regulations in the interest of long-term sustainability.

India's hill resorts have already suffered seriously from a lack of concern for their carrying capacities and the unchecked influx of tourists during the summer months. If India's forest sanctuaries and pristine beaches are not to suffer the same fate, attention will have to be paid during the Tenth Plan obtaining regulatory and public support for sustainability concerns.

Factors affecting the long-term interest of tourism:

— Lack of community participation and aware-ness of benefits.

— Lack of involvement of the rural sector Lack of concern for sustainability.

The Tenth Plan Strategy

The Tenth Plan strategy is to work towards a national consensus on the role of tourism in national development and to focus on the removal of barriers that hamper its growth. To make public sector investment more effective, it is necessary to work towards the inter-sectoral convergence of policies and programmes that could benefit tourism.

The New Tourism Policy envisages a framework, which is Government-led, private sector driven and oriented towards community welfare, with the Government creating the legislative framework and basic infrastructure for tourism development, the private sector providing the quality product and the community providing active support. The overall vision of the development of tourism embodied in the new policy will be achieved through five key strategic objectives. These are:

(i) Positioning tourism as a national priority.

(ii) Enhancing India's competitiveness as a tourist destination.

(iii) Improving and expanding product deve-lopment.

(iv) Creation of world class infrastructure.

(v) Effective marketing plans and programmes.

Major components of the Tenth Plan strategy:

— To develop a national consensus on the role of tourism in the development agenda of the nation through the National Development Council.

— To enhance the effectiveness of public sector investment through the inter-sectoral convergence and prioritisation of tourism-related infrastructure programmes in other sectors like special tourist trains, rail and aviation links, rural roads etc..

— To remove the barriers to growth to leverage private sector investment.

— To mobilise the support of the primary players, viz. the State Governments, in tourism development.

— To mobilise public support by creating awareness of the socio-economic benefits of tourism for the host community.

— To provide legislative and regulatory support to protect the tourism industry, the consumer and the environment.

— To involve the rural sector in tourism and start mobile training units for service providers in rural areas identified for the development of tourism.

— To augment training facilities in hotel management and food craft and build the capacity of service providers at the cutting edge.

— To create world class circuits and destinations, eschew haphazard development.

Positioning Tourism As A National Priority

A concerted effort will be made, through the NDC, to arrive at a consensus on the role of tourism in the development agenda of the nation. Inclusion of tourism in the Concurrent List of the Constitution will provide constitutional recognition to the tourism sector and enable the central government to legislate for tourism development.

A proposal to this effect has been circulated by the Department of Tourism to the state governments for comments and has also been discussed at a Chief Ministers' conference and a majority of the states have agreed to the proposal. Other initiatives include the setting up of Tourism Advisory Council with key stakeholders functioning as a think tank and the constitution of a Group of Ministers on Tourism to improve policy integration and co-ordination.

The adoption of a tourism satellite accounting system is underway to gauge more precisely the contribution of tourism to the national economy. A national awareness campaign in order to create a popular movement in favour of tourism is being planned through a professionally managed communication strategy. Most importantly, the efficiency of public investment in tourism supporting activities will be improved through effective inter-sectoral coordination and prioritisation.

General Inter-sectoral Support:

— Indian Railway Catering and Tourism Deve-lopment Corporation Limited becomes functional in 1999.

— Railways to run tourist trains on nominated sectors in association with Government/ private enterprise.

— Competition introduced in telecom service segments, improving communication links.

— Work on the Golden Quadrilateral highway project and North-South and East-West corridors in progress.

— Delhi, Mumbai, Chennai and Kolkata airports to be modernised.

— New airports proposed to be set up in Bangalore, Hyderabad and Goa.

— Integrated development of mega cities and small and medium towns under way

— Pradhan Mantri Gram Sadak Yojana (PMGSY) launched to provide connectivity to rural areas announced in 2000

Enhancing India's Competitiveness As A Tourist Destination

As air capacity available to India is woefully short during the peak travel months, ranging from October to March, especially for the main tourism originating regions such as North America, Western Europe and South Asia, it is necessary to open India's skies to increase capacity and help enhance tourism. Additional seat capacity from the major tourism generating destinations would significantly benefit the national economy and provide a major impetus to tourism. Improvement in the standard of facilities and services at the international and national airports will need to be speeded up by employing professional manage-ment agencies and by privatising and leasing out airports.

To enhance India's competitiveness as a tourist destination, it is proposed to simplify the visa procedures and consider strategies for the speedy issue of visas including electronic visas and visas on arrival. An attempt will be made, through a consensus, to reduce the heavy and multiple taxes that reduce the competitiveness of the Indian tourism product. Special tourism police will be deployed at major tourist destinations during the Tenth Plan to provide security to travellers and promote India as a safe destination.

Issues taken up by the Department of Tourism with the Ministry of Finance:

— Reduction of expenditure tax.

— Rationalisation of service tax.

— Incentives under the Income Tax Act for the tourism industry.

— Reduction of levies on aviation turbine fuel (ATF).

— Waiver of inland air travel tax.

— Rural tourism to get the same benefits as agriculture.

— Part refund of excise duty for luxury buses.

Improving And Expanding Product Development

Product development strategy during the Tenth Plan will be related to the special interests of tourist target markets. Cultural and heritage tourism will be expanded. India has a vast array of protected monuments with 22 world heritage sites, 16 of which are monuments. The integrated deve-lopment of areas around these monuments provides an opportunity for the development of cultural tourism in India.

For the development of beach and coastal tourism, a number of sites on the west coast of India will be identified for the development as beach resorts by the private sector. The sites will be offered on long term lease at preferential terms. These sites will primarily be on the beaches of Goa, Kerala, and North Karnataka because of easier access by air.

During the Tenth Plan Kochi in Kerala and the Andaman and Nicobar Islands will be developed as international cruise destina-tions because of their proximity to international cruise routes and their exotic appeal.

India's unmatched variety of cuisine is becoming increasingly popular in the world and will be developed as a special attraction. It is proposed to create a highly skilled workforce of culinary professionals through an innovative incentive scheme not only for India but also to promote Indian cuisine internationally.

Village tourism will be promoted as the primary tourism product of India to spread tourism and its socio-economic benefits to rural areas.

India's great wildlife variety has not been developed as a tourist attraction. Wildlife sanctuaries and national parks will become an integral part of the Indian tourism product. Priority will be given to the preparation of site and visitor management plans for key parks. The quality of tourist facilities available at the parks will be enhanced after a prioritisation of parks. Tentatively these will be: Corbett National Park, Kanha National Park, Bandhav Garh National Park, Kaziranga, Madhumali, Bharatpur, Periyar, Ranthambore, Little Rann of Kutch, Chilka, and the Sunderbans.

India has the greatest adventure tourism assets in the world in the Himalayas and its rivers. Mountain-based adventure activities will be developed and promoted. Regulations and certification for adventure tourism operators will be introduced so that the minimum standards of safety and conservation are met.

India receives only a minuscule proportion of the global meetings, conventions and exhibition market. It is important that India develops a world class international convention city not just for the sake of tourism development but also for international and domestic trade and commerce.

India's most unique tourism product during the Tenth Plan will be holistic healing and rejuvenation packages. In focussing on this, it will capture the essence of Indian culture for international and Indian visitors alike.

India's fairs and festivals, some of which are already well established such as the Pushkar mela, the Desert Festival at Jaisalmer, the Kumbh Mela etc. will be promoted as unique products of India. The Festivals of India progra-mme will be re-introduced in the top 12 future markets for India - initially with an annual event in the United Kingdom and the United States, to be followed by triennial events in the other markets.

Shopping will be recognised as an integral part of tourism. The development of dedicated shopping centres for traditional crafts desig-ned along the lines of village haats such as Dilli Haat and Shilpgram will be encouraged and information on where to procure specific crafts made available through shopping guides.

Delhi will be positioned as the cultural capital of India supported by an ongoing and vibrant calendar of cultural events. The development of such a niche-based special interest product-mix will position India as a unique and competitive destination.

Creation Of World Class Infrastructure

The need for physical infrastructure for tourism ranges from ports of entry to modes of transport to destinations (airways, roadways, railways or waterways), to urban infrastructure such as access roads, power, water supply, sewerage and telecommunication. This underscores the need for inter-sectoral convergence of infrastructural schemes and programmes that could support tourist destinations.

The road network is vital for tourism as almost 70 per cent of passengers in India travel by road. Many tourist circuits are entirely dependent on roads. The current government plan for the road system in the country covering both inter-state highways and improvements to rural roads directly supports tourism development. There is urgent need to construct and improve highways linking the 22 world heritage sites and places of tourist significance. The Ministry of Road Transport and National Highways will collaborate with the Ministry of Tourism in this effort.

The Indian railway system can also become an enormous asset to the development of the tourism and hospitality industry in the country. The railways hold a special fascination for foreign tourists who wish to travel the country. For the vast majority of domestic tourists also, the railways is the most affordable means of travel linking the length and breadth of the country. Introduction of special tourist trains with pre-set itineraries and private sector participation will be encouraged.

The Indian Railways plan to establish 100 hotels at railway stations to serve specific tourist centres. The private sector will be given incentives to operate these hotels on long-term leases. These hotels will provide clean and inexpensive accommo-dation for budget tourists.

The Indian Railways also owns a number of heritage structures, which, if effectively maintained and marketed, could serve, both as railway stations and places of tourist interest. India has five hill railways, which compare with the best hill railway systems in the world. The enormous tourist potential of these products will be tapped during the Tenth Plan.

As steam-hauled trains like the Royal Orient, Buddha Parikrama, Palace-On-Wheels and Fairy Queen are extremely popular with tourists, steam traction for special tourist segments will be continued. Trains like the Shatabdi and the Rajdhani with a special tourism and hospitality focus will be planned both for foreign and domestic tourists.

India's 7,000-km coastline and her mighty rivers will be tapped for the promotion of cruises. Care will be taken to develop world class tourism products. As the Ministry of Tourism's financial assistance to the states has not been able to have the desired impact in terms of creating of world class tourism infrastructure, the emphasis must shift to the development of specific travel circuits as internationally competitive destinations and the convergence of resources and expertise for these circuits.

The availability of trained manpower is essential to achieve excellence in the tourism sector. At present, there are 21 Institutes of Hotel Management and Catering Technology (IHM&TC) and 13 Food Craft Institutes in the country. In addition, a good number of accredited institutes also cater to the growing demand in the service sector. It is estimated that only 50 per cent of the require-ment of the market is met by these institutes. Five new Institutes of hotel management would be set up in the Tenth Plan – three in the newly created states of Uttaranchal, Jharkhand and Chhattisgarh and two in the northeast. In addition, 15 more Food Craft Institutes will be set up in the Tenth Plan, and efforts will be made to take culinary crafts and training to the rural areas through mobile training units. A new scheme on capacity building to train service providers in the unorganised sector such as small hotels, dhabas, restaurants and other eating joints is also proposed.

Strategy For Effective Marketing

As there is fierce competition for tourists from India's source markets, India needs to change its traditional marketing approach to one that is more competitive and modern. It needs to develop a unique market position, image and brand, which cannot be held by any other competitor. India's positioning statement will capture the essence of its tourism product to convey an 'image' of the product to a potential customer. This image will be related not only to its ancient Vedic civilisation with a cultural heritage that continues to thrive especially in its rural areas but also to its essentially secular nature.

In the Tenth Plan, an extensive market research programme will be launched in the target source markets and tourism products developed to cater to the interests of each source market. An effective and ongoing market representation presence will be established with the travel trade in each source market and an Internet portal set up in various languages to provide information, a description of the product and the product requirements of the target market segments.

The Internet has a great impact on the marketing of travel and tourism. It has already established itself as a channel through which tourism organisations can promote their destinations and products. Indian tourism will utilise both the Internet and other emerging interactive technologies to avail of the benefits to be gained.

The Path Ahead

The tourism sector needs a national consensus on the role and place of tourism in national development and the early removal of impediments that have hitherto handicapped its growth. The Tenth Plan target of the creation of 18 million jobs through tourism requires a substantial investment of Rs. 38,800 crore at the rate of 47 jobs per one million rupees of investment, both from the public and the private sector.

Public sector investment, though limited, can be made more efficient through the inter-sectoral convergence of policies and programmes supportive of tourism. An integrated inter-sectoral investment plan that provides effective infra-structural support to tourism through the Ministries of Railways, Surface Transport, Shipping, Civil Aviation, Urban Development, Rural Development and Environment and Forests etc. can be achieved through the preparation of a tourism component plan.

Private sector investment can be enhanced by removing the barriers to growth and expediting critical policies that are being evolved. Public and legislative support will be essential for the sustainable development of the sector. The success of the New Tourism Policy 2002 will be largely determined by the success achieved on all these fronts.

6

Tourism in Nepal

Nepal is a medium country of 24 million people south of the Himalayan mountain range in Asia. Due to the extreme variation in altitude, it possesses some of the most diverse climates in the world. With these climates come an amazing range of topography, flora and fauna- think Hawaii on steroids. The cultural diversity of Nepal is no different. There are over sixty-five races and tribes — divided and mixed with respect to latitude and altitude into an amazing panoply of human adaption.

Nepal is an enchanting part of the world and many people visit because of what they have heard, seen or experienced. Its economy has several important characteristics. Tourism accounts for only 3.8 percent of GDP but 18 percent of foreign exchange; carpet and textile exports account for most of the foreign exchange. About 10 - 15 percent of tourism revenue goes to the government, the rest goes to 275,000 people in the tourism industry. 80 percent of Nepalis work in agriculture. International aid has a large impact, funding over 28 percent of total budgetary expenditures, 40 percent of public sector programs and/or 60 percent of development.

The tourist economy of Nepal stands on four legs: the Kathmandu valley, site of the national capital, many tourist attractions and most of Nepal's economic infrastructure; Chitwan National Park (NP), a reserve in the Terai formed by removing all its inhabitants; Sagarmatha NP, the park containing Mount Everest and most of the Sherpa population; and the Annapurna Conservation Area (ACAP) - home to over forty thousand people and high peaks - founded in 1986 and fairly successful at managing tourism.

Visualize tourism as a series of markets within markets: hotels compete within competing neighbourhoods within competing cities within competing countries; all seek the tourist's custom. Attractions are on one axis and facilities are on the other. A tourist sees each destination as a vector whose slope depends on its mix of attractions and facilities. On each vector are dots for time (travel to the location) and cost (once at the location); dots which are closer to the origin represent less attractive characteristics.

The tourist chooses between destinations according to their intersections with the tourist's indifference curve(s). Intersections close to the origin are at a lower utility than those farther away so the tourist will select the destination which allows them to be on the highest indifference curve. If there are changes in the time to arrive or cost to stay at a location, the location's attractiveness changes - possibly changing the tourist's choice. If a number of tourists decide against a location, the demand curve of tourists for that location shifts in.

The industry has caused significant environmental impact in the Himalayan protected areas. Its policies in Nepal are dictated by the need to earn foreign exchange;

sustainability of its resources (natural, cultural and human) has been largely ignored. The irony is that other events have given an adverse shock to Nepal's reputation and arrivals have dropped precipitously.

Nepal has had success with tourism, but the market structure is changing. HMG is opening new areas to maintain revenue growth in a market that cannot consolidate. HMG says its goal is development of 'backward' regions. Both of these reasons are puny compared to the numbers in consideration. It is planning for 1.25 million annual arrivals in 2015. This number is five times current levels, over twice current facility capacity and way beyond carrying capacity. To understand how 'puny' these reasons are, consider one recently-opened region (Upper Mustang) which has about a thousand annual visitors, with each perhaps spending $1,000 on their visit to Mustang. Given that backward regions are rare and opening slowly, HMG has not found a solution. Potentially the reason that these regions are being opened is to either create news events for tourism publications or to please development advocates who want to see the tourism industry expand.

There are few, if any, property rights with respect to forest or trees in Nepal. Publicly-owned property can be stolen through stealth, deception, bribery or mere opportunity. Private property, in contrast, is protected up to its market value.

Many discussions of economic policy - macroeconomics aside - boil down to a tension between market allocation and public intervention. If the price of a product rejects its true and total costs, economists say that supply and demand are efficient and that there is no reason to interfere the market. When costs of an activity are not rejected in its price, we say externalities exist. If tourists' firewood supplies cost less than the market price, local people and the environment bear the cost of that externality. This paper is not about that finding, but how various actors with power can and do choose to ignore it - in their own self-interest. Tour operators, tourists and government make larger profits when they avoid externality costs. Economists recommend that externalities be internalized into market prices, which will then act as an accurate signal. Non-economic solutions are ineffective.

The soaring number of trekkers in the high Himalayas over the last decade has created a booming firewood business for some mountain people, but it has grown at the expense of the forests and particularly fragile ecosystems of the upper slopes.

Imperfect information affects demand by changing the perceptions people have of the product they consume and the cost of that consumption. Tourist destinations prefer to not call attention to problems for fear of losing business. Outsiders also like the situation to be good, so they can enjoy a guilt-free vacation. Ographic cited the success of the ACAP in preserving the local culture and environment.

The success of ACAP shifted the demand curve out and increased the quantity of tourists across all price-levels. Nepal says that arrivals to the Annapurna area increased 56 percent after the establishment of the ACAP in 1986. This is not a problem if the demanders of tourism pay the full price of their presence, but it is if their presence pushes a place beyond its carrying capacity. Although the designers of ACAP (who came from the World Wildlife Fund) claimed their project to be a success, failure to consider some economic effects — either by design or implementation—means that externalities persist. ACAP has been more successful at addressing local issues such as deforestation, energy consumption, and water supplies but suffers from the same government policies as other locations with respect to property rights, tourism permits, central government interference, etc.—diluting the gains of its unique structure.

The result of imperfect information is that tourists cannot adjust their demand to reject the damage occurring in Nepal. If they could, the demand curve would shift in, reducing the amount of damage and providing an incentive for HMG and the tourism operators to correct the situation. On the other side of the information market, we may have too much bad news. Researchers and Non-Governmental Organizations (NGO's) have an incentive to keep the situation in Nepal critical, but not quite fatal, so that they can continue to study the problem, publish and justify fundraising and/ or budgetary spending.

The Nepal Tourism Board (NTB) is a National Organization newly established by an act of Parliament in the form of partnership between His Majesty's Government, and the private sector tourism industry of Nepal. The NTB will now be responsible for all the marketing activities aimed at promoting Nepal as a premier destination. Although the initial phase of the functioning of the Board will be focussed in marketing and promotion, the ultimate aim of the NTB is to take over regulatory and product development activities as well. The functioning of the NTB has the commitment and the support of the Government as well as the dynamism of the private sector.

The Board has been created to provide a vision drawn leadership, continuity of promotional efforts, good management and guidance to Nepal's tourism industry. The funds for the NTB will be collected from the entire tourism related businesses in the form of tourist service fee, thereby keeping it financially independent. The Board is working towards repositioning the image of the country so as to market and promote Nepal aggressively and extensively both domestically and internationally. This is very crucial as Nepal, though small in size, has immense cultural and natural diversity and is one of the most beautiful countries in the world. The friendliness and hospitality of the people of Nepal, where guests are treated as Gods; the variety of exciting adventure activities including trekking, mountaineering, rafting and jungle safari combined with culture that epitomizes peace and harmony; art and craft; songs and dances make a visit to Nepal a memorable experience. We feel proud and honoured to welcome you to Nepal.

Mismanagement and regulatory capture are steps on the road to corruption, with increasingly clear results: human talent goes into rent-seeking—not productive enterprize; funding goes to opaque government programs whose results are hard to document and budget easy to waylay—not education and medicine; and capital-intensive resource industries have the greatest concentration of "rent-collectors", since they offer the highest return to effort - unlike agriculture with too many scattered participants. Rapid growth, chaotic political or legal systems contribute to corruption by decreasing the chance of getting noticed or caught; Nepal has all three.

Tourism is vulnerable to corruption. Bureaucrats like it because tourism depends on natural resources and provides a concentrated source of foreign exchange, free from measurement constraints. Tourism operators like it because ever-present bribe-seekers can be paid off with smaller-than-average bribesto reduce taxes - increasing pro fits in two ways. Using public goods and paying a portion of their value to corrupt bureaucrats, guards, or thieves increases profits a third way. The actors in Nepal's tourism market all have their own utility-maximizing functions. Their interactions in the market produce the non-sustainable result that we worry about today.

Tourists will be pleased if cost, travel time and environmental impact are low and if amenities and attractions are high. In fact, costs are very low due to high facility capacity and Nepal's generally low costs, travel time is falling, and amenities are available to suit most tastes. The most important factors for the ecotourists are the attractions (parks and mountains) and their impact. The government and tour operators see the parks and mountains as both unique (attracting rents) and inviolate. If tourists see either the mountains as less pristine or their tourism as damaging, they will either value it less or not undertake it at all, shifting in their demand curve.

It seems that Multilateral Organizations such as World Bank, UN, IMF, etc. and the ten-thousand-plus NGO's in Nepal (MONGO's) have more power than HMG; although MONGO's would find other work if Nepal disappeared, HMG couldn't function without their assistance. HMG receives 28 percent of its budget funding from MONGO's. An increase in the amount of aid caused a decrease in a country's ICRG rating for government quality. The effects of large flows of aid can include displacement of citizen influence on policy as tax revenue declines in importance, widespread rent-seeking, and even, perversely, leaving populations poor so as to qualify for aid. A 25 percent rise in the aid to GDP ratio results in a 3 percent decline in ICRG and 1 percent decline in growth. Donor-sponsored \technical assistance" led countries in the wrong direction. MONGO's provide technical assistance to increase tourism in developing countries because tourism utilizes their competitive advantage (unique nature) to earn foreign exchange.

Foreign exchange can be used to pay for (always popular) imports and keep the current account balanced, as conventional wisdom would recommend. These policies may not be in Nepal's best interest. Multilateral organizations funded both the destruction and (now) restoration of the resources. The mangroves were destroyed for aquaculture-exports. Is Nepal on the same road? The signs are not good. From a political-economic point of view, foreign MONGO's will not advocate ecological conservation if the result is fewer tourists. That result would displease HMG, the tourism industry and tourists from their home country. If ecological conservation fixed a problem (e.g., deforestation), it could even put some NGO's out of work.

Instead of fewer tourists, MONGO's have supported "Fortress Conservation", ie, excluding all people from a park to keep it pristine for visitors. This works when the central government can provide funds but disaster results in the developing world. Local people rely heavily on their local wilderness and cannot be excluded easily without compensation; small budgets do not allow for either compensation or conservation. People in Ghana resent their ecotourism projects (funded by blue-ribbon international agencies) because they are excluded from both decision-making and the protected areas.

The Nepali government, like any other, is complex. We need to keep three factors in mind while looking at Nepal's: first, the power structures between the ministries matter - one may overrule another; second, bureaucrats have the ability to follow their personal agenda - even if this conflicts with their job; third, people in South Asia look to the government to solve their problems; this can augment the forces of inertia and delay necessary change. The Department of National Parks and Wildlife Conservation (DNPWC) is responsible for conservation measures in Sagarmatha NP (and others) but cannot regulate tourist activities in the park, which are the responsibility of the Ministry of Tourism (MT). The interests of these two departments conflict - DNPWC pushes conservation, MT pushes tourist arrivals.

In the bureaucratic paradise of the Soviet Union, bureaucrats in charge of producing essentials won inter-ministry battles, even if the cost was high. In Nepal, the essential product is hard currency. Part of the reason DNPWC has lost is accounting. Parks cost HMG $5 million per year, but tourists only contribute $1 million per year to HMG. This deficit is deceiving; annual expenditure attributed to the parks is $27 million.

Biologists with the goal of maximizing catch may have complete and logical scientific basis for their projections, but completely fail to account for the bioeconomic input costs. Given externalities, more tourists mean greater damage. Although the government acknowledges that tourism levels are at carrying capacity, its policy of opening new areas to tourism in the so-called \backward and underdeveloped" regions adds new destruction while reduces it nowhere. HMG is content to earn foreign exchange in ways that MONGO's like; MONGO's will even pay for the clean-up costs once damage is done.

Besides corruption in regulation, tourism attracts corrupt officials due to its characteristic risk, natural resources, and strong cash flows. Whether or not government officials participate directly in tourism, their incentive is to expand it for prestige, bribes, and/or personal rents . As an industry, tourism is vulnerable to outside manipulation.

Self-interested groups (tourists, tour organizations, MONGO's, HMG, and bureaucrats) who maximize their utilities via power, deceit, and/or hard currency care little about the costs of deforestation. The people of Nepal do face the costs associated with deforestation, as well as some benefits. If this balance changed, it would hurt the more powerful groups above them. Of course, the powerful claim that tourism will be the salvation of the 'backward' poor, but actual facts indicate that powerful loggers are saving the forest by cutting its trees.

The Conventional wisdom is that only a small portion of tourist revenues stay in the local communities These communities then consume resources valuable to the tourists because they are of little long-term value. Ecotourism recognizes this and proposes that locals who benefit from tourism will protect those resources. Taylor et al., curious about the huge migration from mainland Ecuador to the Galapagos caused by this seemingly small benefit, found that the benefits from tourism, after considering multiplier effects, were much larger. So it seems that the local people are finding ways to benefit from tourism but not by enough to appreciably slow resource consumption - Taylor et al. projected that a 10 percent increase in tourism increased resource use by 4 percent. These impacts should make any ecotourism advocate pause - recall that the HMG plans 5 percent annual arrival growth. In the quest or a portion of profits, local people perhaps lose the most for the smallest gain. This statement would be more powerful if we could define the winners and losers—among the local people—more clearly. Although the winners are evident, the losers are perhaps harder to find. Long-term impacts are also hard to measure, if they are even of interest.

When locals participate in ecotourism, their patrimoine becomes a commodity for sale; a sustainable lifestyle changes to an extractive and consumptive lifestyle. In addition, Sherpas working in tourism do not act as stewards of the land or forest - removing a traditional counterweight to resource consumption. Stonich examined the effects of tourism on households, the environment and economy of the Bay Islands of Honduras, which suffer from the same "hot spot" impacts as tourist sites in Nepal. In the Bay Islands, the poor suffer the results of overgrazing, unstable roads, overfishing, freshwater shortage and water contamination. Although they are blamed, these effects are caused by the activities of wealthy ocals and tourists.

The wealthy avoid high fecal counts in the water supply with purified water. These impacts on water parallel the impacts on trees in Nepal, where tourists have much higher firewood consumption per capita. Since wood is overexploited in Nepal, increasing scarcity hurts the poor disproportionately. Poor women spend more time gathering wood. Family welfare suffers. There is some evidence that resource depletion is rational. Locals chop trees to maximize revenue—while the good times last even if they would prefer to have them later—if they were still there. After all, trendy tourists are fickle and may go elsewhere, reducing future revenues based on ecotourism to zero.

7

Sustainable Tourism Development

The tourism industry is characterized by a range of various interests held by a number of different stakeholders. In order for the various groups to resolve differences or conflicts, governments must take the lead in fostering cooperation and collaboration. This can be done by ensuring that the integrated, sustainable features of the industry are kept in mind as all stakeholders express their views and interests, and that decisions are made accordingly. Coordination, management and planning by government agencies are prerequisites for creating the modalities to sustain tourism development and ensure that stakeholders keep in view their collective interests.

Sustainable tourism development requires direct attention and explicit statements with regard to policies and future plans. However, governments in many countries and areas of Asia and the Pacific may face constraints in meeting these requirements owing to limitations in the financial and human resources necessary to carry out responsibilities for policy-making, planning, coordinating and monitoring in the many areas covered by sustainable tourism development. In the face of these constraints, there are two approaches that might lead to solutions. The first is to encourage greater participation and cooperation with the private sector, and the second is to encourage greater regional and subregional cooperation in sharing experience, facilities and costs.

The recommendations of various meetings, seminars and workshops, including the Intergovernmental Meeting on Tourism Development, have shown that there is considerable scope for strengthening national capabilities and promoting regional cooperation in achieving sustainable tourism development.

The rapid growth of tourism can lead to a number of problems that challenge the effectiveness and efficiency of governments in policy-making, planning and managing sustainable tourism development. Effectiveness and efficiency in this area also depend on the role of the private sector and the scope for private-public sector cooperation.

There is a need for a clear mandate from the government to facilitate appropriate roles for the various stakeholders. There is also a need for integrating and coordinating tourism policy-making and planning with the full range of other government agencies, such as those involved in infrastructure, human resources development, environmental management, immigration, border-crossing formalities and social development at the community level.

Both substantive and procedural policy issues which influence the strength of national capabilities were considered at the Intergovernmental Meeting on Tourism

Development. These policy issues serve as the parameters for the present plan of action. Indicated below are some of the major policy issues which need attention.

Tourism Policy

The tourism policy of a country provides the most explicit indication of the governmental approach to sustainable tourism development and the role that all stakeholders in the tourism industry need to play. As part of tourism policy, organizations can be set up which are able to set objectives, formulate plans and implement programmes.

Policy makers need reliable information and good-quality data on a timely basis in order to appreciate the complex and long-term interactions that tourism has to maintain with the rest of the economy. If information or data are lacking, then the importance of the contribution of tourism to sustainable socio-economic development tends to be overlooked.

In many countries of Asia and the Pacific, the national tourism organizations do not receive enough resources, and their capabilities therefore remain limited. Tourism policy and the work of the national tourism organization should be able to emphasize the interrelationship that involves a number of concerns related to sustainable tourism development, such as human resources development, the economic impact of tourism, environmental management, infrastructure, travel facilitation and cooperation at the regional or subregional levels.

Operational planning

Planning has both policy and operational elements which form part of the process by which the government decides on objectives, sets out the means for achieving the objectives and sets priorities. Policy planning involves the long-term outline of general goals, objectives and directions for sustainable tourism development. Operational planning covers the strategies and procedures to be implemented in order to carry out the policy. Integrated planning also requires reliable and timely information in order to highlight clearly the links between national economic development and the tourism sector.

Development of a tourism master plan and introduction of integrated tourism planning are appropriate approaches for sustainable tourism development, because all aspects can be covered in a comprehensive way, including the social, cultural, economic and environmental aspects. A master plan and integrated tourism planning can indicate that the tourism sector is a major part of the national economy and that the planning process will be ongoing and action-oriented in ways that facilitate implementation.

Managing

Managing sustainable tourism development involves leading, coordinating and controlling in order to bring together all of the resources that will contribute to formulating and implementing the national tourism policy. Administrative issues are also involved as they relate to setting up the structure of a national tourism organization and defining its functions and responsibilities.

Leading the development may involve setting up councils or committees at the highest levels of government to underscore the commitment, and being a catalyst for sustainable tourism development. Coordinating may require working with the various stakeholders from the national level to the local level in order to set priorities and create consensus for action.

Controlling may include establishing mechanisms, laws and regulations that ensure coherent intersectoral coördination within the government and that will promote broader participation and spread benefits more widely to sustain tourism development.

Management can also become more effective if supported by systematic, reliable information. Such information can also play a role leading to greater awareness of the opportunities and benefits that could be derived from cooperation and sharing among countries at the regional and subregional levels.

Private sector participation

In most Asian and Pacific countries and areas, the private sector is recognized as a major stakeholder since it is largely responsible for providing tourism services. One of the most important issues has been how to attract greater private sector participation, including development of partnership between the public and private sectors. Several other issues concerning the relationship between the public and private sectors involve creating a conducive business environment, providing investment incentives, having an adequate legislative framework and strengthening the capabilities of government officials in formulating projects, setting priorities and negotiating with the private sector.

Proposals for action

Under the overall framework of strengthening national capabilities and promoting regional cooperation in sustainable tourism development, the plan proposes action at the national level and supporting action at the regional level. In this context, six theme areas have been identified in which specific action is required. The theme areas are:

(a) human resources development in the tourism sector;

(b) the economic impact of tourism;

(c) environmental management of tourism;

(d) infrastructure development and investment for the tourism sector;

(e) facilitation of travel; and

(f) regional and subregional cooperation in tourism development.

Some of the action required in each theme area is indicated below.

Human resources development

Many countries in Asia and the Pacific face the general problem of lacking strategies and policies for human resources development for tourism. The need to develop the required human resources for the tourism industry has become imperative as a result of the rapid growth of tourism. Some of the specific problems which need to be addressed include:

(a) the quantity and quality of human resources which are related to the labour-intensive nature of the industry and the need for a high standard of specialized skills in cross-cultural working environments;

(b) the shortage of tourism training infrastructure and qualified trainers in many countries; and

(c) the lack of national legislation and guidelines to improve the working conditions in the tourism industry.

In this context, the following specific action could be taken:

Action at the national level

(1) Governments should assess present and future training requirements for human resources development.

(2) Governments should consider formulating national strategies for tourism training and human resources development.

(3) Each country should establish a national tourism training committee, consisting of representatives of the government, training institutes and the tourism industry.

(4) Each country should consider participating actively in the activities of the Network of Asia-Pacific Education and Training Institutes in Tourism (APETIT)established by ESCAP in 1997.

(5) Each country should consider setting up a national network of tourism education and training institutes to further strengthen cooperation.

Supporting action at the regional level

ESCAP, the World Tourism Organization (WTO) and other international and regional organizations involved in tourism should extend their full support to ensure the effective operation of APETIT, with a view to promoting human resources development in many countries.

Economic impact of tourism

The net contribution of tourism to the economy is often not known, beyond a general awareness of the economic benefits, with the result that effective and appropriate policies cannot be made. To overcome this problem, reliable, systematic research on the economic impact of tourism is needed.

A realistic assessment of the economic impact can help to make integrated planning easier, strengthen the links between national economic policy-making and sustainable tourism development and enable better understanding of how to enhance the economic benefits from tourism. Countries could also learn how to enhance the economic benefits from tourism by studying each other 's experience. In this context, the following action could be taken:

Action at the national level

(1) Countries which have already made studies of the economic impact of tourism should continuously update their data and research, and use these findings in establishing the appropriate role for tourism in the national economy.

(2) Countries which have not yet studied the economic impact of tourism should initiate action to undertake such research and studies, so to be able to establish appropriate policy for tourism development.

Supporting action at the regional level

(1) Seminars and workshops should be organized to strengthen country capabilities to use different methodologies for determining the economic impact, including the WTO global methodology, tourism satellite account; and WTO could provide its expertise in support of country and regional studies.

(2) ESCAP, which prepared Guidelines on Input-output Analysis of Tourism could assist countries in measuring the economic impact of tourism using the input-output technique, through advisory services or the organization of national workshops.

Environmental management

The problems related to the environmental management of tourism development arise from the complex relationship between development and its impact on the environment. The problems of adverse impacts could be tackled through effective planning and coordination of action, enforcement of legislation and governance. Efforts in this respect should include the issues of coordinating strategies at all levels and among many sectors in order to improve welfare, make appropriate use of resources and create awareness of the environmental consequences.

Problems with legislation relate to the enforcement of laws, the lack of human resources trained to monitor and enforce the laws and the need for stakeholders to understand that compliance with the law provides long-term benefits that sustain tourism. Government agencies need to give more attention to planning, coordination and monitoring in order to achieve sustainable tourism development that includes protecting and preserving the environment.

There is also a need to increase awareness of how the rapid growth of tourism affects the ecology of tourist destinations in many different environments. It thus becomes imperative to find ways to integrate environmental management with tourism development, thereby ensuring more sustainable tourism development.

Greater attention may also be required for environments at special risk, such as coastal and marine environments and mountain environments. The problem of sustainability must also be addressed in terms of balancing tourism development with preserving the environment, the cultural heritage and the indigenous culture of local communities. In this context, the following action could be taken:

Action at the national level

(1) Governments should give more attention to the planning, coordination and monitoring of tourism development and environmental management.

(2) Local communities should have greater involvement in environmental management and sustainable tourism development.

(3) Governments should create awareness through the mass media, among the general public and international tourists about protecting and preserving the environment in order to sustain tourism.

(4) Countries should pay particular attention to the development and promotion of ecotourism.

Supporting action at the regional level

(1) Seminars and workshops should be organized in order to facilitate the sharing of experience and information for developing ecotourism.

(2) Technical cooperation among developing countries should be promoted through exchange visits of experts on technical aspects of the environmental management of sustainable tourism development.

Infrastructure development

There is a close and dynamic relationship between infrastructure development and sustainable tourism development, because inadequate infrastructure is one of the most serious constraints on future tourism development.

To overcome constraints and problems, an integrated planning approach and formulation of master plans should be encouraged. The government should create an environment conducive to private sector investment and provide adequate incentives to that end. In addition, infrastructure requirements for tourism development should be properly integrated with the full range of a country 's infrastructure development and investment requirements. To this end, the following action could be taken:

Action at the national level

(1) Governments should indicate their clear commitment to private sector involvement in tourism

infrastructure development, and this should form part of integrated plans or a master plan.

(2) In order to attract private sector participation, governments should address such issues as creating a conducive business environment, liberalizing rules and regulations, providing investment incentives, developing an adequate legislative framework and strengthening government capacity to negotiate.

(3) National workshops should be organized to build capabilities among government officials in negotiating techniques and in promoting partnership between the public and private sectors in order to develop tourism and related infrastructure.

Supporting action at the regional level

(1) The World Bank, the Asian Development Bank and other development financing institutions should extend full assistance to tourism infrastructure development.

(2) Seminars and workshops should be organized on tourism infrastructure development and investment involving policy makers, investors, national tourism organizations and other government agencies in order to share experience among countries at different stages of tourism development.

(3) Training workshops should be organized to build capabilities among government officials in negotiating techniques and to promote relationships between the public and private sectors for tourism and related infrastructure development.

Facilitation of travel

A wide range of travel facilitation problems could impede sustainable tourism development. These problems may include lack of accessibility by air, road, rail and water transport; inefficient policies and procedures for visas, customs and currency; possible threats to the health and safety of tourists; the lack of information services for tourists; a negative image if there is overpricing; shortage of trained people in the government and the tourism industry; and the complex nature of border formalities and customs regulations. Governments have a direct role to play in making policies, rules and regulations and providing infrastructure affecting these factors. To this end, the following action could be taken:

Action at the national level

(1) Each country should set up an interministerial committee or council, including representatives of the tourism industry, to promote coordinated development of tourism and facilitation of travel.

(2) Each country should consider setting up a consultative council comprising the tourism and aviation industries to consider accessibility issues by sharing views and harmonizing divergent interests.

(3) Countries should conduct training programmes for immigration and customs officials to make needed changes and take the required action in order to improve efficiency and courtesy.

(4) Countries should develop national policies on tourism health and safety and provide tourists with appropriate information upon arrival.

Supporting action at the regional level

(1) Regional seminars should be organized to share experience and learn from the best practices within and outside the region.

(2) ESCAP should undertake land transport corridor studies along major routes to identify barriers to tourist travel and suggest remedial measures.

(3) WTO, and other concerned international and regional organizations, should provide information and training on safety, security and health standards for tourists and encourage countries to share experience in developing a multilateral agreement on safety and security standards.

Cooperation in tourism development

Countries and areas in the region, and different subregions individually, may have limited accessibility, lack resources and/or capabilities or have inadequate arrangements for expanding tourism.

Regional and subregional cooperation could help governments and the tourism industry in addressing many problems more effectively by sharing information, facilities, experience and expertise. Such cooperation would promote sustainable tourism development by conserving scarce resources, increasing cultural and economic understanding and increasing the frequency of international contacts and exchange. Regional and subregional cooperation enables countries to learn from each other, share facilities and reduce unnecessary competition.

Regional and subregional cooperation to promote tourism could be initiated among the members of different regional and subregional groups, namely, the Association of South East Asian Nations (ASEAN), the South Asian Association for Regional Cooperation (SAARC), Asia-Pacific Economic Cooperation (APEC), the Indian Ocean, the Greater Mekong subregion, Bangladesh-India-Myanmar-Sri Lanka-Thailand Economic Cooperation (BIMST-EC), the Tumen River area, the Pacific islands, and among the countries along the Silk Road and the Asian Highway. In this context, the following specific action could be taken:

Action at the national level

(1) Governments should participate actively in the existing cooperative groupings with a view to contributing to regional and subregional tourism development and to benefit from sharing and collaboration.

(2) Governments should take initiatives to strengthen bilateral and multilateral cooperative arrangements for sustainable tourism development and promotion.

Supporting action at the regional level

(1) ESCAP, WTO and other international and regional organizations should make concerted efforts in areas of their special competence to promote regional and subregional cooperation, as well as to strengthen national capabilities in sustainable tourism development.

(2) Some of the mechanisms which could be considered by these agencies in promoting regional and subregional cooperation may include the organization of regional and subregional meetings and seminars and the conduct of studies.

Modalities

The national action and supporting regional action enumerated above provide a clear guide to the specific responses that are part of the action plan. One or more modalities may facilitate the achievement of each action. Governments and regional organizations are encouraged to be innovative and imaginative in preparing approaches which make use of national and regional resources.

Effective implementation of the plan of action will require a fundamental review of policy-making, planning, managing and defining private sector participation for the purpose of sustainable tourism development. A number of modalities are presented in order that the consequences of action will be far-reaching in socio-economic and environmental terms. The modalities suggested for the national level are designed to address the far-reaching socio-economic consequences associated with sustainable tourism development.

Governments would generally be responsible for action at the national level, while action at the regional level can support and facilitate. Supporting action at the regional level may cover technical assistance; regional research and development, including comparative studies; opportunities to exchange experience and know-how; and cooperation and facilitation of sustainable tourism development activities which are expected to have an impact transcending national borders.

A number of modalities are listed below which could enable implementation of the proposed national action.

(a) *Policy coordination committee for sustainable tourism development*: Collaboration is needed at the highest level at which policy is developed, formulated and coordinated. The primary role of the committee could be to provide a framework for integrated tourism planning or master plans, harmonize strategies and propose consolidation of the resources of various tourism-related ministries and agencies in order to attain sustainable tourism objectives in an efficient way.

(b) *Public/private sector consultative committees*: The private sector, including business enterprises and non-governmental organizations (NGOs), are involved in many areas of sustainable tourism development. Consultative committees are one type of modality enabling the government to maintain constructive dialogue and to have multiple sources of information to help in policy-making, planning and management.

(c) *Facilitation committees:* Sustainable tourism development will require harmonious interactions involving parties from both the public and private sectors who need to work together, even when difficult issues may arise, when the needs of various government ministries may differ and when various short-term objectives may create disagreements. Implementation also requires collaboration among various parties and organizations. Facilitation committees are a type of modality for resolving problems and issues at the working level and contributing to improved productivity and reduction in costs.

(d) *Interdisciplinary teams*: People with specialized fields of expertise and experience are valuable resources and can contribute to sustainable tourism development by virtue of the synergy created by their collaboration. Such interdisciplinary teams can be organized for special, time-bound tasks that will contribute to the process of sustainable tourism development.

(e) *Sustainable development zones*: The creation of such zones in different parts of the country provides opportunities to focus efforts and formulate experimental or pilot projects for sustainable tourism development. Development zones allow for innovative approaches and can serve as an experiment before full implementation.

(f) *Demonstration projects for sustainable tourism development*: Before implementing national-level reforms, demonstration projects at the local and community levels can test reforms of legislation, administration and participation related to sustainable tourism development. This modality would work with small-scale projects and activities and could provide useful information if projects need to be adjusted in order to be successful.

A number of modalities can be used at the regional level to play a supportive role or serve as catalyst for the process of sustainable tourism development.

(a) *Sharing of information, research and data*: Information, research and data collected on a regional basis can serve as a foundation for regional cooperation. It should be possible to identify similar types of policies, plans and projects where information exchanges may be useful. Information about educational and training opportunities in all areas of sustainable tourism development could be disseminated throughout the region.

(b) *Comparative studies in sustainable tourism development*: As countries of the region gain valuable experience in the policy-making, planning and management of sustainable tourism development, this experience could provide a worthwhile resource for the region. It is important, however, for comparative studies to be based on thorough and careful evaluation. Where possible, such comparative studies may yield general guidelines based on experience in the region.

(c) *Technical cooperation among developing countries:* A number of countries and areas in the region have had successful experience in the various areas of sustainable tourism development. TCDC is one modality that provides opportunities for sharing experience among developing countries.

(d) *Regional and subregional cooperation*: Given the considerable differences in the levels of socio-economic development reached by countries in the region, it may be possible to find a variety of approaches to sustainable tourism development. This provides a solid basis for regional and subregional cooperation in order to share and compare experience; to provide mutual assistance in human resources development; and to develop regional and subregional policies and plans.

Implementation and monitoring

Coordination and cooperation are the crucial factors for effective implementation of policies, plans and programmes to promote sustainable tourism development at the national level. Such coordination and cooperation are also necessary among international, regional and subregional organizations and agencies which provide assistance to countries, both within and outside the United Nations system.

Governments need to set explicit goals and form implementation strategies at the national level in order to carry out the proposals contained in the action plan. Encouraging the participation of the private sector in the implementation process will create opportunities to identify complementarities of experience, expertise and resources.

At the regional level, all concerned United Nations agencies and other international and regional organizations should be able to contribute to the implementation of the action plan. Joint efforts by these organizations can mobilize assistance to countries and areas of the region. With regard to the time-frame for implementation of the action plan, it starts with the adoption of the plan by the Commission at its fifty-fifth session in April 1999 and continues up to 2005, that is, covering almost two medium-term plan periods.

Inter-agency meetings, ad hoc intergovernmental meetings or legislative committees will provide the opportunity for discussions of regional concerns about issues of sustainable tourism development and keep implementation of the action plan under review. It will also allow redirection as required, so that planned activities and outputs remain relevant to the priority needs of the countries.

Specific, measurable indicators of achievement will be developed and consolidated within particular projects in order to facilitate the monitoring process. Detailed progress reports as part of the review reports prepared on infrastructure and tourism will be submitted to the Committee on Transport, Communications, Tourism and Infrastructure Development once every two years. When presenting progress reports, countries will be invited to inform the Committee about progress with regard to national action. There will also be a consolidated report on activities and outputs produced under the regional programme.

Resource mobilization Strategies

The scale and coverage of the action plan would start with a thorough examination of current practices. Such an examination would help in the implementation of far-reaching proposals for action designed to strengthen national capacity for sustaining tourism development. In this connection, the tourism sector could thus play a more effective role in national development. The potential benefits from the action designed to achieve sustainable tourism development would justify the resources needed to achieve a new type of socio-economic development.

Traditional and non-traditional resources must be mobilized to support the proposals for action at the national and regional levels. Many countries will have to try to mobilize domestic savings, and this effort will encourage support from potential donors, both domestic and international. Extensive resources already exist in the Asian and Pacific region in terms of expertise and experience which could be employed to strengthen national capacity in sustainable tourism development. TCDC could lead to sharing a great number of these resources. The private sector can have a significant role in sharing expertise as well as providing financial resources, and should be encouraged in a wide range of projects.

Many countries will require considerable assistance from national resources, public and private sector support and assistance from international, regional and subregional agencies as well as donor governments. Among the countries that may require such assistance are those classified as least developed, landlocked and island developing countries and economies in transition. Concerned donor agencies and countries need to give special attention to providing financial and technical assistance in order to implement the programmes and projects that are part of the action plan. At the same time, high priority support for implementation of the action plan must be insisted upon in national, bilateral and regional forums.

Bibliography

Alvares, C., *The Transforming of Goa*, ed. Norman Dantes, Delhi: Other India Press, 1999.

____________, *Fish Curry and Rice*, Mapusa: The Goa Foundation, 2002.

Anonymous, *"India Opposes EU Move To Redefine 'Market Access"* Norms", Business Standard, August 21, 2002.

____________, *"Projects Worth Rs 28,921-cr Postponed"*, Business Line, Bangalore, November 22, 2001.

____________ , *"Resistance Building Up Against Recreation Park"*, Herald, August 9, 2002.

____________,*"Tourism Takes a Wrong Turn"*, Deccan Herald, October 12, 2002.

____________, *"What Does the GATS Mean....for India"*, Economic Times, September 1, 2002.

Benavides, D., "The Sustainability of International Tourism in Developing Countries", *Paper Presented at the Seminar on Tourism Policy and Economic Growth*. Berlin, March, 2001.

Chachadi and Kalavampara, *"Degradation Of Groundwater Environment Due to Sea Water Intrusion Parts of Goa Coast"*, 1999.

Chanda, R., "India and GATS 2000: Negotiating Strategies and Domestic Reforms", *ICRIER Seminar Paper*: New Delhi, September 26, 2001.

Confederation Of Indian Industry (CII), "*WTO-GATS Negotiations: Implications for Indian Tourism Industry*", Slides from presentation, 2001.

Fredline, E., and Faulkner, W, "International Market Analysis of Wildlife Tourism", *Wildlife Tourism Research Report Series*, Gold Coast, CRC for Sustainable Tourism, 2001.

Muloin, S.; Zeppel, H.; Higginbottom, K., "Indigenous Wildlife Tourism in Australia", *Wildlife Tourism Research Report Series*: No 15, Gold Coast, CRC for Sustainable Tourism, 2001.

